I0426576

The Consular Investigator

Out of the Frying Pan into the Fire

(3rd Edition)

A Short Novel by

EFREN M. POONN

Copyright © 2014 Onofre Poonin

All rights reserved.

ISBN-13: 9781493513482

DEDICATION

I dedicate this writing wholeheartedly
to the people with whom I loved:
To my late parents, my brothers and sisters
and to all my friends
To my late eldest brother who had been my inspiration
in the pursuit of my goals
To General Saavedra
who has always led us in Prayer before meals
To my nephew, Pastor Jun
who does not stop texting me his Bible Bites
To my beloved wife Emma
who is always there for me in sickness and in health.
To my eldest daughter Leilani
who has achieved her dreams in the United Kingdom
To my four other children,
Lhon, Bimbo, Beng and Jeff
who have always been the object of my endeavors
And to my grandchildren,
Shane, Shaden, Harry, Steven and Bela,
who are the apples of my eyes.

I DEDICATE THIS TO ALL OF YOU!!

Efren

EFREN M. POONN

The Consular Investigator

Out of the Frying Pan into the Fire

(4th edition)

By Efren M. Poonn
For my family and friends, with love.

PROLOGUE

This book came about because of an ill-fated car accident involving a Consular Investigator in the winter of 1992.

"The vehicle suddenly went out of control and it is thrown over the narrow chasm at a height of 30 to 50 feet above the sea level. I'm all shocked at the sight of our actual crash. My mouth wide-opened, my eyes deeply closed and I grimaced in fear. I'm not sure if I'm scared in the face of an imminent death, but probably, it's just my terrified reaction that I did nothing but shut my eyes in terror while cradled by **the arms of the wind**; tense all my muscles in anticipation of my broken dead body, and for a split second, flashed back the memory of my nice olden days with my beloved family. "MY KIDS!" I screamed on top of my voice as the vehicle went flying into the air and down below. The bark of a coconut tree is slightly shaved off in passing. The car hits the bottom of the cliff and turns right-side-down at sudden impact. The sound of heavy plunge breaks the quietude of the place. "CRASSHH!" Then, Silence...

In the beginning.

The Championship match inside the Roman Coliseum is going on. Everyone crowded the dome, obviously to watch the ultimate title fight between myself and Freddie Black. My rank is way down below his **when** it comes to fighting experience, although we are both holding 1st Dan Karate Black Belt and both finalists in the karate championship. Freddie and I stand 5'8 and weigh 145 lbs. I'm two years younger than him. I just turned 24 last June. Clad in white Karate uniform, I've had an average body built, but judging by the looks, I have enough stamina and firm shape for the impending fight, apparently due to my rigid training and difficult calisthenics in the gym. My Karate preparation is compulsory, a pre-requisite for my job as a House Detective in the Hotel. I love this sport so much, that's why I don't consider this sport a hotel requirement. In fact, I have won five stiff fights in various Karate tournaments and this would be my next championship victory, if ever.

My opponent, sporting a long hair and clad in red-black outfit, has a superior body built and a poker face. His Karate uniform could hardly conceal those bulging muscles -- probably because of his ten long years Karate work-out in Mr. Suzuki's stable. Pointing his fuckin' finger on me, he gives a sharp, insulting look at my face. "You're dead!" Spit.

I sure know he had knocked-out nine vicious fighters without difficulty, and this ensuing championship could be Freddie's next victory fight, if ever. I don't fear him anyway.

The referee is standing right between us with his right-hand drawn straight forward, on a frontward-leaning stance -- ready to signal the start of the competition. The crowd as well as karate enthusiasts are all seated round and excitedly watching us. From the look of their eyes, they're just eager to know who would remain standing in the final round. While on the open-leg stance, we both bowed to each other as an indication of the approaching match.

"COME ON!" Fans and spectators could hardly wait. The impending fight rose to a clamor, "FIGHT! FIGHT! DO IT!"

The referee finally signals the tussle. He wields his right hand down to start on -- in the vehement shouting of the crowd.

"FIGHT!"

While I'm about to move my feet to prepare for my fighting stance, Black swiftly executes successive lunge punches and a variety of kicks, obviously to finish me down immediately. He looks as if he couldn't wait any longer. I found myself kissing on the canvass ten seconds before the end of this damned first round. I've been hit strongly in the face, and I'm in a terrible fix before the frantic reaction of the aficionados. My nose bleeds. I fall short of my defense, that's all! I'm stupidly caught barehanded.

Freddie has a stunning speed. His steps and strikes are undiscerning. He is extremely a tremendous fighter, but I'm steadily gaining pulse in the second round. Slowly, I'm on to analyzing his body movements. His rage and ferociousness cause him extra vulnerable to retaliation. I take note of his working errors and timing. I call it "telegraphing". I study his moves and anticipate the combination of punches and kicks that Freddie should perform by looking at slight changes in his facial expressions. I always remember one article about fighting strategy.

"...there is some correlation between facial gestures and body movements. When a fighter lowers the chin to the side *and closes the lips, there are high probabilities that a "hook punch" will be released from that side of the body. A slight lifting or lowering of a shoulder implies that a front kick (mae-geri) maybe coming from that side of the body."*

I consider several lessons about Predicting *Komite* Strategies. And I always follow this method religiously. In the next round, I was able to completely forecast all impending attacks. I can foretell where should the strike flow from. I become aware of his tactical footwork and confusing hand blows. We exchange strong punches, block and counter, butts, elbow strikes, knife-hand thrusts, front and side-kicks, blow by blow, kick by kick and what have you.

As the scuffle goes on, both of us are sweating vigorously. My muscles tensed, my impulses are automatically reacting. Freddie's face shows determination to win at all cost. His hateful eyes are crashing on my face. If his eyes could kill, I must have been killed a while ago. His obvious focus is to knock myself down in one hard, single blow.

Just in time, I take advantage penetrating his counter. As he delivers his front thrust kick to my abdomen, I depress it with a downward crossed block, and in split seconds, I successfully execute one quick reversed roundhouse kick with my heel to his jaw, sending him down below the ringside. He looks dismayed as he droops on the canvass -- surprised. His furious eyes are punishing.

Groggy but obviously fuming, he jumped back from the canvass and attacked in two hefty leaps. "KIYAHH!" Freddie yelled; executing a thundering flying kick to hit me in the neck, but I already anticipate his desperate move. Now I know he's no longer using his head. I leaped higher into the air above his cover, at the same time hitting him back with one spectacular vertical elbow strike to his forehead.

At last, I pitched him down to the canvass and he slumped unconscious for a couple of minutes; brow blood-spattered.

"ONE, TWO, THREE, FOUR, FIVE, SIX, SEVEN, EIGHT, NINE, TEN! The referee has completed the mandatory ten-counts, but Freddie Black remained unmoving. He raised my left arm to announce victory.

"HOORAY!" the crowd cheers in standing ovation. Our referee and the panel of judges draw near; patting on my back. "Good timing huh?" one of the judges said. "It's a terrific fight!"

My name is Ofrey McPoe, my friends in Metro Manila call me, "Bimbo", but my pet name in the province, especially in my hometown is "Efren", what an epithet! I'm a karate-trained house detective in the Hotel. But actually, I have a pending job application with the U.S. Embassy. It's been almost three months now since I filed such an application, and today, my morning is extremely beautiful, not only for winning the competition last night, but owing to Mr. Park who is waving his hand right now to give something particularly exciting.

"Hey Bimbo, here is a letter for you." He was seated in a swivel chair when I arrived in the office. Mr. Park is the Chief Security of the Ramada hotel, and I'm one of a few stay-in security detectives therein. I smiled as I sat on the chair near his desk and received my letter.

"Thank you Sir!". I gazed at the heading, curiously.

"Wow! This mail comes from the Embassy."

"You're about to leave us?" he said.

"Well, Sir, I'm just taking chances."

I read the content; excited and interested.

"We are pleased to invite you for an interview on September 10, 1977 at 8:00am at the Embassy Chancery", the letter said. I was thrilled.

"At last! My job application takes in. ...so glad I can't wait till tomorrow!" I called my colleague's attention to show the letter off, but they looked reticent. I learn later, that John, my supposed friend, simply mumbled when I left the room.

"I wish you'd push off!" Noemi, my co-employee heard that words and babbled on later.

The Embassy building is majestic in its stately location alongside the shoreline of Manila Bay. Its frontage is easily seen just a few meters away from the thoroughfare although partly covered by acacia trees on a well-maintained blue grasses. It is surrounded by high concrete and iron railings with wide vehicular and pedestrian gates as well as security concrete barriers. The gates are manned by two security guards staunchly standing in blue and white uniforms, with short firearms properly tucked in their black holsters. One of them is holding a metal detector in his right hand, ready to carry out the so-called "under-chassis inspection." There's a large parking space in the medium portion of the facade which is intended for employees and official vehicles alike.

Two clean-cut U.S. Marines in complete military uniform are standing in the lobby. A lady Receptionist is in the booth.

"Good morning. Can I help you, Sir?"

"I'm Mr. McPoe." I show her my appointment letter.

"Can you tell Mr. Tan I'm here?"

Mr. Tan is the Personnel Officer of the Embassy who has a hand for my interview.

Please wait for a second," she dialed.

"Hello, Mr. Tan, Mr. McPoe is here in the lobby," her eyes fixed on my face.

While waiting, I can't help but have a quick look in the entire lobby. "The Chancery Mail Room is located in the left corner near the office of the Cashier. On the right side is a large twin-door leading to the ballroom, with ornamental base and a country flag on its side. There's an expansive stairs within the left side going to the Personnel Department, where I'm heading on for the interview." After a while, Mr. Tan arrives at the lobby door through the stairs. He is a Filipino, about 40 years old, with a small body built and sporting casual look. He takes a quick look at the waiting area as if he is after somebody, and he finally caught sight of my presence.

"Mr. McPoe?"

"Yes Mr. Tan?" I stood up.

"Please come!" I walked with him going to the second floor till we both reached the Personnel Office.

"Have a seat," Mr. Tan begins. "I'm going to give you a typing test and written exams." He walks to a nearby office table and put some coffee in the cup, blended with a small amount of sugar. He also prepares a piece of pancake.

"Before we begin, please take your coffee first," he hands me a coffee cup and pancake. I'm amazed. "Great, I have a free coffee break while going through my tests."

The interview and written exams went on. Paper tests followed and I went through with all my exams a few hours later.

"You have passed the tests," Mr. Tan smiles. "The next thing for you to do is to undergo physical exams," he gave the medical referral.

"We will see if you are physically fit to work. Please present this letter to the Doctor and I'll keep you informed with the result!"

"Thank you so much Sir!" I said softly. I open my mouth as if to speak further, but I'm at a loss for words to express my gratitude.

"I can't believe it," I told myself. "I would soon be working with the embassy? It's great!"

I walked down the expansive stairs of the chancery going to the clinic clutching my medical referral. The Medical department is located in the backyard of the chancery on the second floor near the Friday Club -- a place for the marines to linger on during relaxing hours. Dr. Jude, the lady physician in white uniform is in, seated on the swivel chair facing her table while apparently writing some notes. Her office is obviously complete with medical equipment, from X-ray apparatus to the smallest tools. There's a bed portion for the patient to lie down and to undergo examination, covered by a green curtain about an overhead length.

"Good morning Ma'am!" I greeted her; presenting my medical referral. Dr. Jude stood up from the chair and casually received the letter to read.

"Alright, let's see." She stared at my face as if she's gauging my physical condition.

"So, you're an applicant for the Treasury Department?"

"Yes Ma'am," I nodded.

She pulled on the medical drawers above her head

reaching for the stethoscope.

"Okay, let's start with your physical test."

The aim of the medical exams is to select, for a particular post, a person who must be in good physical and mental health and must be free from any physical defect or disability that is likely to interfere with efficient standard of the duties and safety of the environment, people, machinery or co-workers. In details, any person seeking appointment in the U. S. Embassy, whether permanent, temporary or deputation basis is required to undergo medical examination. The Pre-employment medical examination is a part of the selection procedure of a candidate for a particular post. Dr. Jude is the authorized Medical Officer, the competent authority to certify a candidate as medically fit. She reserves the right to re-examine or review a medical report.

"You'll be notified of the result," Dr. Jude said after about an hour physical examination.

"Thank you again, Ma'am! 'see you later," I told her with an undiscerning reaction.

For me, working with the embassy has been my long time delusion. It's my life's precious moment. I don't want to just break this dream with such a negative medical finding. I went back to the hotel at my service quarter. I feel heavy in my heart. I have this fear of failing the test. I always sigh deeply as if I've lost my confidence. For one, I have a history of pulmonary ailment when I was a young boy. It is traceable in the X-Ray test and it is going to fail me. I feel depressed!

For almost a week I have not stopped praying, and I prayed really hard hoping for the best and preparing for the worst.

"Hey, Bimbo, you got a mail from the embassy!" John informed me; I was in my room mending my things.

"Thanks John, hand it to me, please!" I'm really keen to

see the report. I smell bad news.

"Oh Lord, please spare me with this one! I am too much worried about the result, my dreams are a bit big, please don't let it bog me down."

John obviously shares with my gray thoughts. He also feels my anxiety, and he's all curious about the letter from the embassy. Is it a notice of my failure? or otherwise? I'm really troubled at the thought of rejection. I was opening the letter by fits and starts.

"Hey, Bimbo, why don't you just open it?" John reminded me once more. "Let's see what's in there."

I nervously opened the letter, slowly, my hand shaking, then I read the entire contents.

THE PAIN OF REJECTION

Chapter 1

A Dream to Keep on

The information is distressing.

"Your X-Ray finding shows an undetermined activity."
"We regret to inform you that you are not fit to work," the letter blows up into my head. I'm startled that my fingers are all thumbs and I let fall a cup of coffee from my hand.

"CRASHED!" so went the sound of a broken cup.
I feel as if heaven and earth collide on me. All along I'm earnestly praying that everything is alright, but now my hope is gone. I can't understand why my intensive prayers fail.

"How come my prayers fall on deaf ears? Jesus, what else have I to do now?" I moan with pain in my heart as I lightly shove my fist on the table.

At 12 o'clock midnight, I went up to my desired praying place at the penthouse flat.

"I must talk to God to beseech for reconsideration," I told myself.

My sub-consciousness is dissuading me. "Yes, and pigs are gonna fly!"

In the middle of the night where all bulb lights in the penthouse are turned off, I do the sign of the Cross as I usually did in the past. I start praying on my knees; slowly moving around, with my arms flatly stretched sideways -- eyes closed.

I lament to God. "Lord, I asked for your intervention and yet I failed my physical exam. I'm asking now again for your benevolent mercy."
I stayed on the rooftop for a straight three hours praying

without let-up, then I felt my hair gradually standing on end. Apparently, my prayer was intense that I was able to perceive a strange flapping of the wings.

"WHAPP, WHAPP!"

"Huh? ..'must be an angel coming down on me!"

I can't bear opening my eyes. I get goose bumps. Terror wraps my skin.

"I'm scared I got to go now. I must let go of this place at once."
Instead of finding the source of the flapping sound, I fixed my eyes on the floor and rushed back downstairs.

"I'm afraid to see supernatural," I told myself.

I don't know if it really holds onto myself with a strange thing on that picky time-–where I am all alone in the badly lit space, on the utmost top of the building with nothing but the shapes of water tank and machinery.

"What is that thing? "Is it a bird or an angel?" I gasped.

"Maybe it's just a product of my pure imagination."
Probably, I bring this odd experience into a dream. While sleeping I saw from nowhere a mysterious figure coming towards me. With indistinct face and low but esteemed voice He said, "Go find your previous employer and proceed to the Medical Unit."

"What for, old man?"

"Ask the nurse for your medical history and whatever you need."

"Then, what?"

"Then take it to the Embassy".

"..and then?"

"Present it to the doctor."

Right after these words, I was wide awake. I glanced at my wristwatch. "It's just 5 a.m. and I just slept for two hours." I looked bleary-eyed as I fixed my eyes on my bed-mates snoring soundly."They are deeply sleeping," I yawned; slightly stretching my arms up. A few cocks crowing intermittently. It's just I who's fully awake as my dream left a deep mark in my head.

"God has obviously shown me the road to take." I told myself.

"I have to go see the company doctor now." (What I'm gearing up is the medical unit of the Deity Motor Corporation, my previous employer.)

I jumped on the floor to prepare for an early bath. I know the medical rules in that company. "The medical record is always treated confidential. It is hardly given to anyone without due course. And little did I know what's in store for me out there. But I think trying my best wouldn't do me any harm."

I merely allayed my concern into remembering my dream the preceding night. It's such a divine initiative that I have to undertake once and for all. I'm desperate that I have to beg if that should be the case. I hope that the company doctor should soon have a change of heart, and he's gonna help me after all. I should really ask for all I'm worth towards getting my records.

"Whatever happens, I have God's help to fall back on," I told myself; preparing to leave.

"So, you are applying for a job in the Embassy," Miss

Jennie told me. She is the resident nurse of the Deity Motors.

"Yes, Ma'am, and I need my medical history records badly."

"Why?" she is looking straight at me.

"I'm going to submit them for medical comparison with the Embassy.

"And...?"

"You see, Ma'am," I narrated my experience." my x-ray finding in the embassy showed undetermined activity, that's why I failed the exam." Jennie was keenly listening.

"And last night, I was told in my dream to visit your place to ask for my medical history. It supports my health status for sure."

The nurse pondered for a moment; slightly nodding her head as if she's weighing the situation.

"Okay!" She said after awhile, "No problem. I won't turn you down," a little smile on her face lessened the seriousness of the problem. It really calmed me down. Jennie's a little bit cute anyway.

"Thank you Ma'am," I said; obviously surprised thus my eyes are twinkling for joy. "you're a big help to me."

"Please have a seat and wait till I find your file." Jennie told me.

"Good heavens! I never thought this should be that easy! My last night's catnap just turned out right. I feel as jumping over the cloud!" I raised my both arms and head as if to fly.

It's 8 o'clock the following day when I knocked at the Embassy's Medical Office. I was tightly carrying a big brown envelope in my right hand containing my X-Ray film and other data taken from the Deity Medical Unit. Doctor Jude was already in, and she opened the door.

"Good morning, doctor!" I greeted her with a vow to show my respect.

"Yes?" Dr. Jude looked hesitant.

"Ma'am," I said meekly; reaching for the file. "I'm bringing my medical record from my previous employer. I want to present this to you for further evaluation."

I handed her the big brown envelope. She gave an alternate look, to the brown envelope, and to my face again.

"Alright," Dr. Jude said in a while.

I thanked God she did acknowledge my file and casually put it on her office table.

"I... I always go to church and pray, Ma'am," I told Dr. Jude. Unconsciously, maybe, I was trying to edge a point into her soft spot.

"Alright, I'll see what says in this plate later."

So far, Dr. Jude accepted my supporting documents without delay. All the while; I was hopeful that Dr. Jude should take my medical history into consideration before finally turning me down. "NO!!" I wished things should be going quite well, by and large.

At exactly a week after the submission of my medical history, I received a letter coming from the Embassy's Personnel Department. It is a notice of my final medical analysis -- a last report that makes or breaks my dreams.

A BREAK CAME INTO PLAY

Chapter 2
The Miracle of Prayer

"We are pleased to inform you that you have passed the medical examination. Your employment with the Department of the Treasury is going to be September 22, 1977 at 7:00am. Please report to Mr. Richard Meyer for orientation."

"Good gracious!" I almost jumped for joy. "I've had the chance of a lifetime! Thank you Lord!"

Nevertheless, my fleeting happiness suddenly brought me to a halt. Something is worrying me. For one, it's already Friday afternoon and four-days are just left till Tuesday, that is the start of my employment -- saving Monday that is an official public holiday. Three days are not enough to prepare for a new atmosphere.

"Where should I stay in the City? Where should I find food for my daily needs?" The question lingers in my head. "In my detective work in the hotel, I enjoy free board and lodging. I have a free quarter to stay. I always eat regularly as the ration for security personnel are simply provided by the kitchen men."

"Of course I should have more decent pay in the Embassy." I'm talking to myself. "But how am I going to survive during the first month in my new job; I am broke till my first pay day?" My own remarks argue against my chance for the office. I should do something to get rid of this problem anyway.

"I have nothing to get from my security agency because of huge cash advances I made during this month."

"And if ever, the agency should surely hold whatever

amount I have the moment it discovers that I'm going to vacate my job for good." But I won't fall out with my conclusions. It is not a good idea to argue with the facts. I just scratched my chin.

"Then where on earth have I to go?" I stare at the sky, and I remember Mr. *Poindexter* quoting about the sky.

"I stood alone beneath the stars and shouted to the heavens at the top of my lungs and what was indeed beautiful was the way the stars shined when the sky swallowed my name."

Then I find myself again scaling my way up to the penthouse of the hotel. Just as I did before, I'm crawling around the empty space with my bended knees and open arms; reciting my prayer all over again. I repeatedly invoke my newest needs from God.

"Please provide me at least a month sustenance to keep me going, Lord!"

And, again, I never refrain from praying till I break my eyes in tears. I enjoy the sense of the blessings God has to give me. I do enjoy receiving His charitable hand at the end of my prayer to see that with what God has given me I have been able to return a gratitude and my faith. I enjoy speaking with God at the solitude of my own heart. I enjoy visiting the rooftop of the hotel and hanging out with the Lord through my earnest prayer; though He has nothing to ask from me except my faith and my humble trust in Him. As I finish my prayer, I slowly make the sign of the Cross and then go down the ground floor by the stairways.

Below the last step of the stairs, I notice a small bundle

of money on the floor partly hidden beside the big ornamental base. It is tightly wrapped with a rubber string.

"Oh, Man! This bundle must have slipped out from the chest pocket of a guest," I presume, "and didn't notice it." I quickly pick it up and turn my head around to make sure nobody has seen me. Then I casually hide myself in the nearby corner of the floor and curiously untie the bundle of money to count all of it.

"One hundred fifty nine dollars!" I burst.

"This money's good enough for my basic needs till I get my first month pay. I still have spare cash to rent for my bed space."

But my mind and conscience are arguing down my decision to hold it back.

"Too bad you asked help from God but you're coveting the money that isn't yours," my heart said.

"God gave me this money," my mind argues.

"Go back and return the money to someone who owned it."

"No! I need it to start my life anew."

I'm totally puzzled if I should surrender the money or keep it for myself. If I should give it back to the real owner, I should also give up my hope for my future. I don't want my best effort to turn to a broken dream. Indeed, when I chanced upon the hard cash awhile ago and actually had it in my hand, my monetary problem has been totally resolved. I weigh my tact. "What if I won't give this up?" I'm staring at the bundle of money in my hand.

BY LEAPS AND BOUND
Chapter 3

Making the Best of it

I finally decided to keep the money for myself.

"God will surely understand I'm sure He will."

The following Tuesday I arrive at the Treasury office at 6:00 a.m., about an hour ahead of time to report for my orientation. Other employees subsequently arrived in succession, and Mr. Meyer, the boss, opens the treasury door at exactly 7:00 am.

"You're going to do all the clerical works in the operation and to assist Cruz in the Mail Section, Mr. Meyer points out in his orientation. I am keenly listening.

"You're also going to deliver volumes of checks to the Central Post Office every afternoon," he added.

"Yes Sir, I'll do it all with pleasure!" I nodded.

I have at last come into my own as an employee of the Department of the Treasury. Ever since I knew that such a stepping stone should allow me to bring all my talents into play. And I am not wrong. My diligence and attention to every job details have eventually produced outstanding result. No joke. For the span of eight months I twice get Special Achievement Award from the Treasury Department. Although I'm not as extroverted as some of my colleagues I am every bit as professional and dedicated. Indeed, my introverted quiet façade is the perfect cover for my quick, analytical mind. My office-mates are getting closer to me in a friendly way, including Mrs. Lora, a 40 year-old married woman who happens to be my immediate supervisor.

"You should apply for the vacancy," Lora told me.

"There's a vacant opening for a higher position in the Treasury. Rhodes gave up that job to settle abroad."

"But Ma'am," I said, "Cruz has long been aspiring for Rhodes' position. He'd resent me if he won't get hired!"

"You just apply for the position, I don't want Cruz promoted. I displease his performance in the Mail Room. He's even arguing me whenever I give him some instructions."

"But Cruz ,"I said, "he has longer and better experience than mine."

"Why? Lora said, "Don't you like the job?"

"I just don't want to hurt him," I told Lora.

"Don't you like a two-step salary increase?"

"But I'll come out a bad guy in Cruz' eyes," I insist.

"Never mind him! Just think about the opportunity first. I want you there. I can persuade Mr. Meyer to give you the job. I will recommend it to him!"

"But Ma'am...

"Do as I say, and stop arguing!" she blushed and walked away. I was left behind scratching my head.

Following Lora's instruction, I applied to the vacancy and the days flew fast.

"Congratulations, Bimbo!" My co-employees offered greetings a week after I got my promotion.

"You are now our treasury's Check Custodian, well done, Bimbo," Mr. Meyer said.

"Oh, thank you, Sir. Thank you, everybody!"

"I told you so!" Lora whispered to my ear.

"How about a blowout?" Vicky, the assistant supervisor,

teases while shaking my hand.

"Oh yeah, you should paint the town red!" Florence seconds in jest.

Everyone is pleased of my new position aside from Cruz. Seated near beside the inserting machine, he is obviously disappointed to hear that his application for the vacant post did not work at all. Even more disappointing that I have come out a winner instead of him.

"Mr. Meyer didn't even consider my long working years in this office." Cruz lamented to Vicky one time.

"I know Lora's behind Bimbo's promotion, and to my frustration," he said.

"How do you say that?" Vicky asked.

"I heard her one time talking to Mr. Meyer, she's discrediting me while she's commending Bimbo," Cruz stressed.

"Bimbo's a hardworking employee anyway," Vicky said.

"And why is that? He only started working last year!" Cruz bursts.

"Oh, oh! Come on Cruz, there's always a chance for everything," she said.

"That will never happen as long as Bimbo is here!" Cruz blasts while standing up suddenly from his chair.

I have just come back from delivering parcels of checks at the central Post office. Unwary about the topic of conversation, I draw near Cruz and Vicky and sit down beside them.

"Hi Cruz, may I borrow the ledger of mails, please?" Cruz slaps with his words. "Better look for yourself!" Apparently, he is getting on his nerves. He drags his pen on the table, leaving Vicky and I in the mail room. The two of us display a surprised look in our eyes. We both stood up to walk back to our cubicles, but Cruz unexpectedly rushed back.

"FUCK YOU!" Cruz suddenly threw a right punch meant to my face.

"HEY!" I was surprised. Impulsively, I was able to dodge his blow and thereafter twisted his wrist in defense. We wrestled on the floor. The chairs went flying. The glasses on the table splintered under the heavy scuffle. Volumes of checks prepared for delivery tumbled and scattered on the floor. Our office mates are taken aback.

"What the hell!" Lora screamed. Mr. Meyer's door bursts open and he rushes into the scene. Seeing him, I impulsively release my grip while Cruz dashes out to the exit, blatantly abandoning the workplace without a word.

"What's goin' on?" Mr. Meyer said.
In the heat of the moment I explain my side.

"He threw a fight and punched me in the face!" I said.
Lora butted in, "I saw Cruz threw him the first punch."

"What's wrong then?"

"Cruz resented his disapproved promotion, and he's blaming it to Bimbo," Vicky told Mr. Mayer.

"He's a troublemaker, you know," Lora said, "he doesn't give up the day job either."

"Alright then, 'back to work. Be sure all checks are intact," Mr. Meyer told us. We help each other picking up the scattered pieces of checks and put back broken chairs in their original place. That's the last time we saw Cruz in the office. He failed to report for work since then. The last bit of information I ever heard of is that Cruz is working in Saudi Arabia.

While I continue my work in the Treasury, I come across with the news that the Consular Section at the ground floor is in need of a new staff, and Mr. Meyer approached me one time.

"Hey, Bimbo! I heard from the Personnel Department that you're applying for the Consular job."

"Yes I did Mr. Meyer."

"Are you willing to leave your work here?"

"I'm after the greener pasture, Sir, if you'll allow it," I meekly told Mr. Meyer.

"Well, if you're going to leave, you won't be able to receive your Christmas bonus and additional benefits. It will be forfeited and you'll start all over again." he warned.

"I'll risk the possibility, Sir", I said.

It's the first week of December when I become a member of the workforce of the Anti-Fraud Unit, an investigative body within the Consular Department. Everybody feels the prickly cold gusty wind as Christmas day is in the offing. And it pleases that I receive my Christmas bonuses and 13th month pay, contrary to what Mr. Meyer has said before.

The office is located in the ground floor of the annex building fronting the corridor and the Visa Section. Inside the carpeted and air-conditioned office shows cubicles of five investigators in a row, facing the desk of the lady secretary. There are two adjacent rooms occupied by two Vice Consuls who are appointed Chief and Deputy Chief respectively.

Close to the corner is a foreign flag, fittingly complemented by a few diplomatic portraits on the wall. I become one of five investigators who conduct office and field investigation and assigned to investigate illegal syndicate. I interview visa applicants and witnesses to establish identification, legitimacy, or their identities and filiations through functioning as Screening Investigator in the Consular.

I also conduct well-organized investigation in the metropolitan area and the provinces. I monitor closely a log of cases in order to assure the expeditious handling of referrals and prepares a list of cases and itinerary for provincial assignments. I have at last come to my own as a valued investigator of the consular and at no time improving my career extremely quickly. It's my dream come true! My neighbors so with a few popular people in my town respect and admire my profession. I suddenly become friends with my former detractors and critics. My kith and kin gradually multiplied.

Unknown people begin to visit my house and introduce themselves as my missing relatives. That's how my life goes on. Even policemen and government officials used to visit us in the house. I fully developed into my own lifestyle and generosity.

"You're too generous and open-minded to your friends, you better watch out," My wife Emma sometime reminds me of my extravagance. "Why, I'll not be like Ofell, your niece. She's selfish and heartless. She only goes after money. She couldn't care less. She is the last person I would think about when it comes to money.

I always remember a quote to fit with Ofell,

"The only gift I can give, is the ability to receive. If giving is a gift, and it surely is, then my gift to you is to allow you to give it to me."

Back to my job.

My fact-finding method is the rule of the game. As an investigator, I should determine if a visa applicant does not willfully misrepresent facts in order to obtain a visa or other documentation.

One complicating case is about a person named Charlton, an immigrant visa applicant, who has a pending visa petition as an unmarried son of a U.S. naturalized citizen. Charlton's submitted documents are under study by the Anti-Fraud Unit. His record looks as if he is qualified for the required single status; he is already a widow with two children. His submitted documents comprise, among others, the required birth certificates of his two kids, an authenticated marriage contract with his wife Daisy, and the latter's death certificate that shows her death in the Northern Province. The place is Charlton's claimed address on his visa application.

I did some verification of records within the Local Civil Registrar of his claimed town. I find in this office that all his submitted civil certificates are duly registered. I also find their marriage contract authentic, but Daisy's death certificate appears to have been late-registered. I ponder,

"Why late?" It appears that Charlton is covering up something.

THE FIELDMAN'S WORKS

Chapter 4
The Troublesome Fact-Findings

I decided to visit his home address. To my surprise, the house does not belong to Charlton. It is occupied and owned by a certain Cooney, who introduced himself as Charlton's olden friend.

"..and where is Charlton residing now?" I asked Cooney.

"Well, I don't know. He rarely comes in this house, "Cooney said.

"How did he manage to receive all call-in letters from the Embassy when in fact he is not residing here?"

"By phone," Cooney said. "Charlton used to call up to check his mail. If there's one here, then, that's the only time he personally comes in for it.

"Why did he use your own address and why did you subscribe to his idea?"

"He just asked if he could use my local address and I said yes. I'm not interested to ask him why and for what. Maybe, he's a traveler, that's why." Cooney said.

"You don't know him well, right?" I said.

"We only became acquainted last year."

"Are you familiar with his wife, Daisy?"

"No! Not really, but I know her name!"

"Where is he residing now? Is Daisy still living with him?"

"Charlton said she's already dead. He's a widow now," Cooney said. His reply fits with the information given on Daisy's Death Certificate.

"Where was his wife buried?"

"Well, that I don't know!"

I did my usual neighborhood assignment. I asked anybody else in the neighborhood about Charlton's whereabouts, but no one else could give the answer I want. There are two possibilities; they are just ignorant of Charlton's personal circumstances or they have been earlier couched to reverse the information. I perceived that Charlton should be hiding something, somehow, somewhere.

"After all, why is he covering up his true address? Probably, he is not a widow and has the nerve to tell a lie just to qualify him for a single visa status. I think it over. "But how can I prove it?"

I went back to my car and just about to hop in when I noticed the wheels; two of them are having flat tires. Obviously, they are intentionally flattened by an "arrogant asshole" who has nothing to do with himself. I looked around scratching my jaw. "Who the hell...

There are some people around closely watching my car from the roadside. One of them displays insulting smile on his face. I tried to ask for a hand but they all fall away. This is not the first time I have this experience. It also happens in the other part of the region for several instances. I know all the while the reason behind. There are some disgruntled visa applicants around the area whose applications have been turned down. For them, the investigator is a turncoat, betraying his fellow Filipinos.

At home, I retrieved all Charlton's documents and carefully studied all entries on his Marriage Contract including his kids' birth certificates. His eldest son's shows a former address in Albay and the other child indicates a given address in Romblon, both are located in the far-flung provinces. I persistently followed all these directions to prove that my perception is correct. While our ship sails going to my destination in Romblon, a storm occurs in the middle of the sea with successive roll of thunder and lightning, strong waves overflow our ship and flood the entire deck, forcing the vessel to sheer off course. Passengers and their baggage as well as the ship crews haplessly slide against the balustrade of the ship, an innate obstacle to save them from sure drop to the deep sea. It continues pitching up and down on the rough water. Children are crying for their mothers, mothers crying for some help and I was firmly holding on the guide rail, gearing up to swim for survival if necessary.

This ordeal continues for about 5 hours till the sea calms down and the big waves gradually subside. I've been able to finally reach my destination before high noon -- to my frustration.

"Charlton's no longer residing here, we don't know where his family is now," neighbors in Romblon said. It's the same story I acquired from the neighbors in Albay when I went there prior to Romblon.

I went back to reviewing all of the documents at home. Charlton's marriage contract shows his marriage to Daisy in 1965, about twenty years ago in Manila. Her given address is "No. 1187 Int. Curbing St., Manila." A former address I have once overlooked in the course of my scrutiny. Gathering new lead, I hastily proceed to the place. I find it a little bit tough to enter the dampened corridor. It's slippery, dim and narrow with too frequent turns. On both sides are shanties and dilapidated concrete walls filled with abstract graffiti. Some bystanders are suspiciously staring at me while I pass by a store.

"This is the interior." At last, I arrive at the target.

"Excuse, Mister, can you tell where is Number 1187? I asked the lone man fixing a bike.

"Well, my house is No. 1182, you can just count up to the fifth house," he said.

"Do you know this fellow?" I show him a close-up photograph. The man put on his eyeglasses and takes a close look at the picture.

"Ah, he is Charlton, but he's just left for a stride. His house's just a few meters away from here."

"Is his wife there?" I said.

"Oh, yes, maybe!"

"What's her name?"

"Daisy." I take a deep breath of relief.

"Whew! At last, I find her!"

"KNOCK! KNOCK!" I was standing beside the second step of the stairs leading to the front door. The door went ajar and a matured woman takes a look.

"Hello, Is my friend Charlton in there?" I slowly wave my right hand.

"Oh, Charlton went to the mall for a while," the woman said.

"By the way, may I have your name Ma'am, if I may ask?" I' was trying to test her response.

"Daisy," she said. She comes out behind the door; mending her two kids.

"So.. you're Charlton's wife -- my best friend?"
Daisy looks strangely at me. "Yes." she said softly. She looks speculating, her eyes fixed on my face as if trying to recognize who I am.

"I have Charlton's picture here and yours too," I move upstairs, preparing for the pictures to show.

"Please sit down," Daisy said; preparing a chair.

"Charlton is handsome in this picture, isn't he?" I move closer. "How is my friend now?

"He's alright," Daisy said.

"Is he a nice husband to you?" I was making a gambit, but Daisy asked back instead.

"Why do you have my husband's picture, and mine too?" She is obviously getting suspicious.

"Well..." I did not waste time answering her. For all the wasteful incidents I came across trying to locate her, it's about time to introduce myself. "I'm from the Embassy," I told her without a blink.

That words obviously went off into Daisy's ear. She slowly becomes pale and stunned over my unexpected introduction. Her knees tremble as if to fall; her eyes centered on my face. She's taken aback. And yes, she's not dead, in contrast with her husband's claim in his visa application. Evidently, Charlton has fabricated his wife's death by presenting a death certificate. He willfully misrepresented facts about his civil status to qualify him for the required single status. And obviously too, Daisy knows it all the while, even to the extent of conspiring with her husband's fraudulent claim in order to obtain a visa. At last, I finally discover their true location, and Daisy, Charlton's wife, is actually talking right now.

"So, the deceased is still breathing, huh?" I said sarcastically.

Daisy's knees slowly bend as if all her strength fades off. Her hope is gone now. Her husband's dream to migrate to the United States and to file later a petition for his family is eventually destroyed. There's nothing left now but their spirits walking beneath the ruins of unfulfilled dreams.

"Sir, let me tell you this," Daisy said in a tensed voice. She starts explaining why and how they arrived at this mess.

"I have to admit I conspired with my husband. I want him to pass the immigration requirement -- for the sake of our children, for a greener pasture in the U.S. and, if God permits, to live there happily ever after. We have sold all of our properties including agricultural farm, house and lot, farm animals and other belongings in the province. We anticipate immigrating to the foreign country someday -- that's why we are only renting a unit in this hidden and stinking part of the community. And after all these discoveries, should we then return to the province with our heads down and nowhere to live?"

Probably, she wants to say more. But she's at a loss for word to speak further. Her physical being is subdued by a rapid trembling of her body. She is too nervous that both her legs slowly bowed down and she suddenly collapsed on the wooden floor, in the presence of her two kids.

"Mama!" cried the children, frantically hugging and shaking their mother, trying to revive her consciousness.

I was taken aback, though I immediately took Daisy in my arms and carried her to rest on the nearby chair. Neighbors rushed in for help.

Give her some fresh air!" a voice said.

"Give her some water!" I exclaimed.

Charlton suddenly appeared from nowhere with a glass of water in his hand and worriedly served it to her.

"Daisy! Come on, get up," he was softly tapping her shoulder.

"Dad," one of his kids called him; coming closer.

"What happened to your mother? What made her collapsed?" Charlton asked his kid with his eyes focus on Daisy.

"She's talking with him when she suddenly collapsed," the girl's eyes go straight to me. Charlton turns his head and he is apparently surprised when he figured out my presence. He remembers me very well. He knows I'm the same investigator who interviewed him in the Anti-Fraud Unit. I was the one who received all his required documents. After all, he knows very well he could no longer make another lie this time.

"Sir," Charlton is still mending his wife who is slowly gaining consciousness. "How did you find us?"

"Well, it's my job to find the truth," I told Charlton.

"I beg your help, sir," Charlton is edging his way to my chair.

"It's our last chance to survive. We have sold everything in the province and we have nothing more to fall back on. Please have a heart, don't turn me down." He is begging for compassion. And Daisy, she is also sobbing silently. The children are sadly looking at us as if they understand the heartache.

"I'm sorry Charlton, I can't make any promises. I'm only doing my job," I said.

"Can I offer you $1,000 dollars just to let me go? He said. "Well, it's not a bribe, sir, it's just a show of our gratitude" Neighbors are keenly listening.

"I just told you, I'm not in the position to decide," I said. I feel my heart affected. I understand very well that the future of this family is now at my fingertip. If I can help, I could cite in the report that I've been able to prove that Daisy is really dead; that I have verified her duly registered death certificate and it's authentic. That's all, and so, Charlton could go.

But how about my loyalty to my job?

"NO! I shall never be a turncoat. NEVER!"

I simply say goodbye to the couple. I do not want to listen further and get carried away to influence my conviction.

"To be loyal to my job is to allow myself to work faithfully, confront my challenges as if to strengthen me further. The only thing I am for sure is my loyalty to my dream, and this means I'm growing, and not stagnant or shrinking."

As I walk back to the main street by the narrow and dilapidated pavement, two rugged men block my way and confront me. The man in brown jacket is holding a baton and the other, a fan knife.

"He caused Daisy to collapse," the man in jacket tells his companion.

"Yeah, you're the stubborn investigator. You're a turncoat! You're betraying your fellow Filipinos," he shouts at me while pointing his forefinger.

This is a hard accusation to live with, but I would not abandon my loyalty to the embassy in the face of this harassment. I prepare my fighting stance, nervous but firm.

"I don't want trouble, men," I told the guys.

"YOU'RE REALLY IN TROUBLE NOW," one of the men said.

"WHIZZ!" The baton strikes downward but I've been able to duck and swiftly move sideward with my right knife-hand, blocking the attacker's right arm. He strikes me again with his baton meant to my head but I have blocked it again and locked the attacker's arm. The other guy rushes in to join the scuffle and stabs me with a knife at my rear. I execute a back-thrust kick before the knife lands on me. It sends the attacker back to the concrete wall. More muggers rush into the scene, ready to pinch me down altogether. I jump over the fence and run for my life. The group follow suit through the pathways. House owners hastily close their windows and lock their doors because of the commotion. Not even one dares to call the police. The residents are breathlessly peeping through the tiny openings. They are curious to see what would happen next. In the close corner, I tensely knock hard on one door to seek refuge but it remains unopened. Residents see me but no one dares to give me a lift. The group is coming nearer and nearer. I am helpless. I have nowhere to escape. The passageway going to the main street is already being watched over by a few members of the group. There's no other way but to fight back and defend my life. The group simultaneously attack me and I defend myself as much as I can. I was able to hit back at them. Everyone I retaliate with my kicks and punches tossed to the ground.

But what could a lone man like me do longer in this situation? I'm not a superhero and I can't defend myself anymore.

I had several kicks and punches all over my body. I was finally beaten black and blue. Two of them pulled me up with my armpits and one of them lunged another hard punch to my ribs.

"AHH!" I groaned in pain. The other guy I fought beforehand rushed to me with a knife intending to kill me. He is fuming. I can see it with my weakened eyes.

"YOU SON OF A BITCH!" he bends his elbow to stab me right in the stomach.

ALONE WITH THE DUMB LOYALTY

Chapter 5
The Rebels

"HEY, BUDDY, STOP!" I heard one voice shouting right before the assailant pierce his knife.

"Charlton?" the group looked back.

"Why?" they asked Charlton.

"He doesn't do you any harm, guys, does he?"

"He turned you down!" a member of the group said.

"Daisy collapsed because of him!" .

"No! Please, he's just doing his job." Charlton walks closer to me.

"Release him," he told the group. The men looked at each other. Nobody moves.

After a while, two guys holding me in the armpits hesitantly released their grips and let me fall down the pavement.

"Hey, Jake," Charlton called a young man standing beside me.

"Help me, we'll carry him to my house", Charlton said.

The young man timidly complied and they take me back to Charlton's house. The muggers are left behind shaking their heads.

"He's a fool!" the leader told the group, and they begin to fall away.

Charlton mends my cut on the left eye shortly as we reach the house.

"Sir, you better take a hot cup of coffee first," Daisy told me. She extends her arm to help me hold the cup. One of her kids offers me a pair of slipper.

"Thank you," I softly told Daisy while clinging onto my memory..

"If not for Charlton I should be dead by now. Or maybe he secretly instructed the bystanders to beat me up and then he would simulate his help. That way, I should be softened and should consider his request."

No. That's not true! The Filipinos are particularly hospitable. They don't expect reciprocation. That's the Filipino way. The group should have just gotten the wrong idea about me.

After a brief rest, Charlton escorted me to my car in the main street. I'm still groggy and weak. The standbys fixed their curious eyes on us while we are walking through the place of scuffle. Nobody dares to speak.

"Thank you again, Charlton," I hopped in the car.

"Don't mention it," Charlton waved his hand a bit. He never mentioned anything about his visa. He lets me go away without a word.

A week after the incident, I received a phone call in the office.

"Good afternoon, Mr. Poe," it's Charlton.

Right Mr. Charlton, can I help you?

"Sir, I hope to say it again. I have $1,500 dollars with me for now. It's part of the payments from my sold properties. We have nothing to turn to at this point in time. There's no turning back. It's all yours, please accept my apology!" the voice on the other line is begging for sympathy. The words are softly delivered but they are deafening into my ears. His supplication touched my heart and went through my soul.

"I will let you know, 'bye!" I told Charlton; just to end the conversation.

For three consecutive weeks I used to receive constant calls from Charlton, over and over, same topic, same request. He was very insistent, and I was beginning to lessen. Unmindfully, I start contemplating what should I do to help him.

Four months have passed by and I did my report on Charlton's case by fits and starts. In fact, I don't want to make an account about Charlton. I have completed all other cases aside from this one. I wanted to wait for my sympathy to quiet down, for if not, I should still be carried away by his plea. I'm not prepared to turn him down at this early phase.

"Hey, Poe, what takes you so long?" Now, my boss is asking me. "Ah..well, Sir, I'm still finalizing my report."

"Can you submit it to me as soon as possible? The visa section is asking for it."

"Err..ah.. Yes, Sir. I'll submit the final report tomorrow morning."

"You better finish it off tonight and have it ready on my desk first hour in the morning." My boss is getting impatient.

I don't know what to do. I am torn between my loyalty to the embassy and my gratitude to a fellow Filipino. I owe Charlton my life. I should write a favorable report for him. It's easy for me to circumvent my story so that Charlton could finally leave the country for good and stop pestering me. But what about my loyalty? My integrity?

Sometimes the decision is hurting. But it should be executed in all honesty, there must be no truth bended. My strong fidelity to the embassy thus dictates that I must write my report as truthful as I can. I'm now ready to make my decision. I work my pen. I set my electric typewriter, I confine all evidences, and then I get through with my findings.

"Mr. Charlton fabricated his story by claiming that his wife is already dead. He even supported it with a death certificate and submitted the same to the Anti-Fraud Unit. The investigator's finding is contrary to his claim, since it has been duly established that his wife is still living with him in the same roof together with their children. Attached is an affidavit of admission signed by him and his wife. Having proven this, he is therefore unqualified for his applied category as unmarried son of a naturalized citizen." Part of my report said.

That was the last time I thought about Charlton. I feel vindicated. After all, it's my loyalty to my job that matters -- an allegiance to the embassy that could go beyond refute. And for Charlton, I'm sorry.

Apart from the sheer number of cases that I must handle, the difficulty of investigating these cases must be emphasized. It often requires that I travel long distance of hundreds of miles, over rough terrain, and into the areas that are either controlled or infiltrated by elements of the insurgency.

"This case has been kept hidden in the investigators' drawer for a long time, it's about time you investigate this case," Mr. Kenny said; handing me the case folder.

He was talking about an immigrant visa case of one

Nicolas Santos, a 67 year-old naturalized U.S. citizen who married an 18- year old girl named Maryann. The wedding was held in a remote area of Cagayan Valley.

Apparently, the rumored presence of some insurgents in the area caused the other investigators to refuse investigating the case.

"It's turned over to me, because I'm more desperate than the rest of my peer group." Well, I was just joking.

Unarmed and alone, I proceeded to Cagayan Valley for a neighborhood and background investigation. The rough and steep elbows of the narrow, mud-spattered roads and a kilometer wide river added me some difficulties reaching the community on purpose, but I still fight my way through the river, by a 20-piece bamboo float rowed by two men; good enough to carry the weight of my car.

As I reached the shore, I heard an intermittent gunfire. I asked a young boy carrying some pieces of wood for fire.

"What's going on up there?"

"There's an ongoing struggle between the rebels and military soldiers across the bridge," the boy told me. He speaks very calmly as if the sound of firing is just an ordinary thing for his ears.

"That's where I'm going to," I told the boy.

"Hey, wait!" I reach for the pictures of the petitioner Nicolas as well as MaryAnn's, and show them to the boy.

"Do you know these people?"

The boy nodded.

"Where can I find him?"

"Across the bridge."

"Are these two people related?"

"Yes," he twice nodded.

"How?" I want to ask what kind of relationship.

"This old man is the grandfather of this one," the boy pointed his finger to the picture of the girl.

"How do you know that?"

"He's my grandfather too," the boy said and walked away.

I took a brief rest in the shade of the tree waiting for the gunfire to subside.

"What would I fear for? I'm not doing wrong," I told myself; preparing to proceed to my destination..

About two kilometers away from the petitioner's house, I conducted some neighborhood inquiries. I was able to confirm from several informants that MaryAnn is indeed the granddaughter of Nicolas the petitioner, who married her in a civil wedding ceremony. I decided to confront the couple in the house.

After a long discussion, Nicolas finally gave up, and confessed that MaryAnn is indeed his granddaughter.

"I married her to help her qualify for the visa petition and eventually go to America," he said.

I gave him a piece of paper and my pen to write the affirmation. "Don't worry," I said, "there's still some ways for her to immigrate to the U.S."

I exchanged talks with the couple to comfort them, and maybe, just to pass the time, then I bade goodbye.

Two men followed me in my car parked underneath the shade of a tree.

"Hey, buddy; I'm Ben, a cop."

"Oh, Hi!"

"Is there a chance for MaryAnn to go to America?"

"Yes," I said, "but she has to change the category she's applying for. She could use a non-immigrant visa instead."

"No." the cop said. "I mean, she could go if you'll make your report favorable to her. After all, we're all Filipinos." He secretly inserted a couple of crumpled cash into my hand.

"No," I said, "I can't accept that. I'm just doing my job."

"Don't you want to be my friend?" the cop insisted the money; exposing the pistol in his waist.

"Well, I'm sorry." I whisked his hand and turned back to hop in the car.

"YOU SON OF..." seemingly annoyed, the cop pulled out his gun and aimed at me, but his companion grabbed his arm to pacify him.   I drove my car off without looking back, leaving the two men behind.

It's getting dark and I was still driving along the treacherous terrain.
I want to rest for the next day drive back home but nowhere can I find any public house to while away the night. As I go along, I see a lumberjack coming out of the timber yard.

Hey, boss, can I spend the night in there?"

"Where are you from?"

"I'm Jeffrey Poe, from Manila. I can't find a traveler's inn for me to stay."

"Oh, Well, come in. I'll introduce you to the manager."

I parked my car in the yard and followed him to the dining area to meet the manager.

"Hey boss, this is Mr. Poe."

"Hi, sir, I'm from the U.S. Embassy."

"Oh, I guess you're a Consular Investigator!" the manager said, "I can see it by your look."

"Yes, I am."

"I'm John, and thank you Mr. Poe," he said; shaking my hand.

"I don't know if it's you who worked on my father's visa papers last year. But I'm very thankful to anyone of you who favorably resolved my father's application. He's now a U. S. immigrant."

I did not find it hard to convince John to let me stay in the lumber house. He offered me a separate room at the second floor and then referred me for some foods in the workers' canteen. Several workers are there eating their meals. A food attendant served me one big plate of brown rice, with chicken soup and vegetables. It's an extremely large meal. I guessed each meal could fill about three or four persons' stomach, but obviously, it's just a simple, ordinary meal for the hard workers.

I've had enough, so I proceeded to my room right after dinner. I was really tired and I wanted some rest. I was sleeping soundly when a successive knocking of the door awakened me at around midnight.

"KNOCK, KNOCK, KNOCK!"

Who's there?"

I was heavy-lidded; I extended my arms to reach the doorknob and slowly put it ajar. Five rugged-looking men holding long firearms entered the room and accosted me. I gained complete consciousness.

"Who are you? What are you doing in this place?" one of them interrogated me. By their looks and manner of questioning, I immediately recognized who they really are; rebels.

"I'm Bimbo, of the U.S. Embassy."

"Why are you here?" one of the rebels said while grabbing my arm. I know I'm not in the right position to resist.

"I'm here to help your town mates -- to resolve their visa problems," my voice is a bit shaky.

"COME WITH US," the leader said.

I tried to resist, but the rebels are quick enough to seize me by the neck. At gunpoint, I was hogtied and taken out of the room into the lumber yard.

"DOWN ON YOUR KNEES!" the leader said; aiming his long firearm to my forehead. The rebels circle round me as I slowly kneel down.

"YOU'RE IN THE INTELLIGENCE!" one of the rebels said.

"No, I'm not," I speak in upset voice.

"I'm a plain consular worker," I said. "I come to this place to work on your town mates' visa application, that's all."

"And what do you mean by that?" the leader said.

"You see," I try to explain, "I came here to do background check for some of our fellow visa applicants who happened to reside in this place. I have to make some reports for them, for if not, their visa application will not move on. It will remain stagnant in our drawer, and they won't be able to get their visas."

"Since you're working for the embassy, you're infiltrating into our territory," the leader insisted.

"NO! Please!" I tried to stress my point. "I'm just helping our town mates."

One of the rebels is feeling annoyed. "That's bullshit! We better finish him off to play it safe," he told the leader.
I sensed an exaggerated danger for my life. I tried to reason out further. I want to edge my way into their soft spot by stressing that I am one of their fellow countrymen. .

"We're both Filipinos," I said. "we must help each other."

Ridiculously, I am now saying the words that somebody has always told me in the past; a common expression of all my previously investigated visa applicants - - something that I always ignore because of my dumb loyalty to the embassy and to my job. Now, I never know whether or not this loyalty can save my life. The embassy that I respect so much is not even aware of what really happens to me in the field.

"Alright, say farewell!" The leader cocks his M-16 rifle and aims at me. His forefinger makes contact with the trigger of the gun; slowly squeezing it to blow my head off.

I tightly close my eyes; waiting. I have no choice but to prepare to die.

A NEVER-ENDING DANGER

Chapter 6
The Infiltration of an Alien Smuggling Syndicate

"WAIT!" the lumberyard manager said. "I'll take him into my custody."

Obviously, John is familiar with the group; owing to his position in the lumber yard.

"I have something to tell you," John puts his hand on the leader's shoulder and walks abreast with him in the dark corner. They both talk seriously for about an hour. I see John's hands gesticulating all along, perhaps, emphasizing his point for my sake. Sometimes John is slowly walking back and forth, maybe, he's trying to explain and convince the leader to let me go. I hope so. Every now and then, John and the radical leader are turning their eyes towards my location.

Several minutes flew fast. The leader finally beckoned his men, and they began to fall away.

"Thank you for the heart!" John told the rebels; waving his hand at the departing group. He subsequently released my strap and escorted me back to my room.

"Thank you very much," I told John. "You save my life."

As I recall, two fellow Filipinos have just saved my life. First it's Charlton who rescued me from the street maulers. He's the same guy whose visa application was turned down because of my honest-to-goodness report. Now, it's manager John who just sets me free from the rebels' ferocity. Without John's intervention, I would surely be dead by now.

I wish there's some way of showing my gratitude to these

fellow countrymen for what they have done for me.

I have just arrived back at the Anti-Fraud office the following day. "Hey Bimbo," my boss is calling me.

"Yes, Mr. Kenny," I peeked through his office door.

"Come in, sit down," he said. "Let me show you something," He is laying a set of passports and Immigrant visas on his desk. I take a seat beside him and pay attention to the materials on the table.

"Can you perceive the difference?" He is pointing on the two passports. I hold the documents trying to compare one passport to the other, the fiber, the entries, the signatures, the seals, the photographs, front and back cover, and the entire pages.

"I can't see the difference," I said. "They just look the same."

"NO! One of them is a phony!" Mr. Kenny asserted.

"How?"

"You better take a close look," he holds one dark brown passport. The inside page shows complete identification, the name, nationality, passport number, gender, date and place of birth, and the signature."

He slowly removed the top plastic cover of the identification page. The ID picture sticks on the plastic cover while completely removing up the exterior coating,. It reveals the original ID picture on the second layer.

"See?"Mr. Kenny said. "This is simply a case of photo substitution!"

"The entries are all genuine except the substituted

photograph of the scammer," he said. "The original owner of this passport is a victim of an alien smuggling syndicate;" pointing his finger on the stuck picture. All victims for that matter pay the syndicate a large amount of money to get their own fraudulent visas regardless of genuineness as long as they could slip out of the country.

Mr. Kenny took the immigrant visa from his desk and handed it to me.

"Take a look at this one; this is a bogus document too."

"How is that?"

"The Vice Consul's signature is forged. Dick Kane is the man behind it. He's the leader of an alien smuggling syndicate, the man with a golden hand."

"Uhuh," I nodded with interest.

"I have a special assignment to you, Bimbo. But before I tell you the details, I want to make sure if you are willing to accept the task."

"Why, yes sir, I'm willing."

"Okay, here is the detail. You're going to accompany an informant to infiltrate Dick Kane's den. You're going with Lucy, our asset."

Lucy is a twenty five year-old woman who introduced herself as a member of the Intelligence group.

I remember her. She's the sweet spoken lady who has a golden brown complexion with matching dark brown hair. In all fairness, she's a bit of fluff.

I lapsed in silence; wondering why of all five investigators, I've been chosen for the task. I should have known better.

"Well, are you chicken?" Mr. Kenny said, apparently testing my willingness..

"No, no!" I said. "I can do it".

"You have to go there without any identification with you. But mind you, that's too risky. You must disguise like an old-fashioned countryman who aspires for an immigrant visa. You should talk to the leader of the syndicate. Convince him that you're badly in need of the visa. They will tell you the fees. So you must assure him that you will pay for his service. Lucy will help you elaborate, do you understand?" .

"Yes, I do," I assured him.

"You shouldn't tell this assignment to anybody."

"Yes, Sir!"

"Not even to your wife, not even to your mother. This is a covert operation, understand?"

"Yeah, Mr. Kenny."

"..And one more thing," he walked through the door.

"Whatever happens to you, this office doesn't know you. Is that clear?"

"Yes, Mr. Kenny!"

Well, I am just paying a lip-service. I don't have any choice. If I should say no, the Chief should say I'm such a coward investigator and should discredit me as well.

"I'm doing this for the sake of the service", I always tell myself.

Lucy and I planned our surveillance at an exclusive house in Makati.

"First, we would check-in at the nearby hostel across the subject house," I suggested.

"HUH? Lucy stared at me; surprised. It didn't escape from my keen senses.

"Yes, but don't worry, I'll behave like a gentleman." I told Lucy. "I have some respect on you. It's nothing but business." After some explanation, I was able to convince her to check in.

"Oh, okay."

"We'll prefer one room at the third floor of the inn. The windows should be facing the under-watch building. It must have a clear view of all activities in the house."

Lucy is a bit reluctant, but she agreed to check in with me on condition that there must be *"no monkey business"*.

"Room No. 311," the bellboy handed me the key and we both went upstairs. We kept watching in rotation through the windows. There are some people around, coming in and out of the house. I want to make sure if Dick Kane really stays in that place.

"It's already 9:00pm and I'm starving now," I told Lucy.

"Let's have a break then, I'm hungry too," Lucy said.

"Do you think we should call up the Reception downstairs to place an order?" Pause. "..or let's just go downtown and have a dinner in a music café, what do you think?"

"Alright!" she said.

The waiter gave us the menu while seated on a bistro's dining table at the downtown Makati. A crooner is on the stage rendering beautiful love song.

"It's not the pale moon that excites me, that thrills and delights me, oh no, it's just the nearness of you," so goes the

song. The crooner has a voice quality very pleasing to the ear. I called for a drink.

"Hey, waiter, give me a bottle of beer."

"Do you like some beer?" I told Lucy.

"Just once," she said.

The love song went after the other, and another, to the pleasure of the listeners. My beer also went after the other, and another, to my own drinking pleasure. The songs hold some appeal for me.

"Shall we dance?" I asked Lucy who is slightly tipsy.

"Okay!"

I was as elated as I danced with her. She's kissable, so beautiful in her silky dress. And what about me? Well, I'm a good-looking young man in my sporty attire. We're just a good fix.

We're passionately staring at each other on the dance floor, wordless, only our feelings could talk.

What said those two people like us communicating through the language of the eyes? That's more perfect than that of the lips, and the soft music in the air is gradually pulling my arms tightly round Lucy's hips until my chest finds contact with her breast. Lucy let escaped a deep sigh. It seems she's as well being drawn by a strange, uncontrollable impulse within herself. She lets me kissed her lips while the sweet music goes on.

Finally at the last hour, we find ourselves lying on the bed inside the hostel room--both naked.

"Oh! Just do it Honey," Lucy whimpers. She stretches both legs apart. Her face pinkish, her head turns upside-down on the bed edge. A pillow is laid flat on the back of her hips.

The room thus becomes the mute witness of a non-stop sexual encounter wherein both Lucy and I savor the ecstasy of such an inadvertent love affair.

"You're really that good, Baby," I whisper to Lucy's ear while my hips are coming up and down against hers.

At 8:00 a.m., Lucy and I are both standing at the front door of the watched house.

"Are you sure he's there?" I'm asking about Kane.

"Oh yes, I've seen him coming in with his car this morning," Lucy said. "This is Kane's den, indeed."

The house is quiet and inconspicuous. The wooden main door is slightly covered with a variety of ornamental plants, with an old private design on top of the door frame, and a peephole over the hub, enough for people indoor to sneak a look once a visitor calls from the outside.

"BUZZ!" the doorbell sounds as Lucy presses the push button.

"What do you want?" the voice said in a miniature speaker.

"We're visa aspirants," Lucy said.

"You've companion?" the voice asked, obviously, he sees me from the inside.

"He's a visa applicant too," Lucy said.

"Do you have an appointment?"

"No, Not at all."

"Okay, give me your names and contact numbers and we'll call you back for the appointment," the voice said.

"Oh, No," Lucy sneered.

"We don't entertain walk-ins," the man said.

We realized that we must abide by their rules; otherwise, we won't be able to get inside to see Kane face to face. Lucy wrote on a blank business card, "Prissy Doll and Dan Simon," and slipped it into the small opening.

"Okay," here's our names and contact number," she said.

A hand emerged and took hold of the card.

"Wait for the call until tomorrow. You must say your pass before you can get in," the voice said.

The two of us walked abreast towards our car. It's a bit long walk to the parking area, and we're unaware of what's going on behind us. A man is rushing behind for Lucy's handbag.

"GOT IT!" The rascal snatched her bag and sprinted towards the secluded area where two scoundrels laid in wait.

"MY BAG!" Lucy screamed as I gave chase. I cornered him in the near turn and the rascal stopped to face me-- preparing for a fight. Before I knew it, and before I could get closer to him, he whistled to his two companions and there they came for aid. The snatcher threw Lucy's bag to the pavement and pulled out a knife.

"YOU FOOL! Who the hell are you to interfere?"

The three are all holding knives and have me cornered. I stand firm on the ground while keenly observing their moves. I'm estimating their fighting response--the time and speed I should need to be able to retaliate.

In split seconds, I swiftly execute an undiscerning front

kick to the snatcher's solar plexus.

"KIYAH!" the man slumps back to the sidewalk and accidentally bumps his head against the walkway casing.

In one continues execution, I deliver one more sharp sidekick to the next companion and he knocks down in pain. An upward knee-kick to the other guy follows and I hit him on his jaw.

In ten seconds, the fight is over. I pick up Lucy's bag and casually walk back to the parking area.

Three days passed by before we got a call from Kane's man, as well as the given password. We proceeded to Kane's den the next day.

"BUZZ!" the doorbell sounds.

"What do you want?" a voice said

"Pizza pie in blue!" Lucy answered, it's the password. The wooden door creaked as it slowly opened, and a man in dark sunglasses emerged through the entrance.

"Come in," the man said.

"Why, you're giving a hard time to applicants like us? Lucy said.

"We're just being cautious," the man said in a low voice.

"Is the boss there?" I asked.

"Yeah, he's inside!"

The man led us into the lobby, close to the stairs.

"Please take your seat, I'll tell the boss," he told us and went upstairs.

We are left in the lobby anxiously waiting. There are other people inside sitting along with us, probably visa aspirants too, or Dick Kane's bodyguards. Security men in civilian attire are standing at every corner of the hall with bulging pistol in their waists. In a little while, the man who escorted us shows himself up behind the balcony's handrail.

"Come with me," he beckons and we follow him upstairs. We walk abreast towards a large isolated room to meet the boss.

"Mr. Kane?" I asked.

"Yeah, please sit down!"

Lucy makes the introduction and we shake hands.

"Mr. Kane, I'm Prissy and this is Simon," Lucy is pointing to me while we are seated on the chairs before Kane's desk.

"He wants to get a visa," she said.

"I see! So, you want to go to the U.S.?" Kane said.

"Yes I do, can you help me?" I said.

"Oh yes. I can get you a visa but, it needs some steep service fees to make things possible."

"Yeah I know, "Prissy" has just told me."

"By the way, from where are you, Simon?" Kane asked.

"Well..." I'm about to respond but Lucy butts in.

"He's residing in Graceland Subdivision, in Pampanga."

Her opening takes Kane by surprise., and me too. After all, I'm not a resident of the place, and I'm not prominent with Pampanga dialect. In fact, I'm living in a province where our people converse in the Tagalog vernacular. But that's what Lucy said, and I should play for it.

"Oh, that's my residence too, how come I have not seen you there?"

I lapse in silence. I'm now roping for an alibi.

"Well, I'm a newcomer in that place," I told him before

long.

Kane looks directly at my face, he seems skeptical at my answer. I know somehow I can be burned out anytime just for a single slip-up of the tongue.

"Anyway," Kane takes away his eyes from me as if he doesn't mind at all.

"Okay, here's the deal," Kane gets his pen and a notepad to write his plan. "I'll give you a visa. I mean, I can make you a visa but you might pay a bit high for the service." I'm keenly listening, nodding a bit.

"You must understand that this doesn't come directly from the Embassy. I'll make it for you." Kane seems estimating my capacity to pay.

"Anyway, it will look as genuine as the original. It's hard to tell which is which," he said. "Your visa will be supported by all vital documents and a photo substituted passport. You don't have to worry about the immigration officers at your point of entry, our contact-guide will be there to pick you up." Kane assured me.

"In case you get caught and deported..." he paused for seconds.

"..we will get you a free new travel documents, and an escort will go with you at the immigration area to ensure successful entry."

That's exactly what Mr. Kenny told me earlier, and Kane is all the while convincing me at the moment. I just act the way I should do, in accordance with Mr. Kenny's instruction.

"Okay, it's a deal," I said.

We are still talking things out when we hear

commotion from the ground floor area, followed by firing of guns.

"BOSS, A RAID!" a bodyguard suddenly barges in while shooting back at the pursuers. Kane's men are fighting back with the lawmen at close quarters, and the raiders are obviously gaining on them. Without a word, Kane quickly runs to a hidden exit and lost from sight, leaving the two of us in panic. We take cover under the slabs to avoid being hit, while exchange of gunfire continues. I see a bullet hit one of Kane's men and he falls flat down the ground floor, over the two dead bodies slumped at the midpoint area. The barrage of bullets continues. We stoop between the exchange of gunfire, running our hands up and down to cover our heads as if bullet would not pierce the surface of the flesh. In the midst of the trouble, I remember the secret door to where Kane has made his way out.

"Come on, RUN!" I told Lucy. I grasped her hand to lead her to the exit, but before we could reach the secret door, a stray bullet hit Lucy at the back, and her hand holding mine freely lets go.

"LUCY!" I turned around to lend her a hand but two successive stray bullets foiled me from doing so.

THE ACCIDENT

Chapter 7
In the Face of Death

The shot nearly hit me; just about an inch enough to penetrate my head. I realize I could no longer help Lucy in any way. The situation dictates that I need to take cover and run off for safety. I run for my life, without Lucy with me, and I'm really sorry.

I find my way out leading to the next building block and safely drive my car back home. I never heard of Lucy since then. I lost track of her; no contact. Morning news never mentions her name. and she has never shown up either. Everybody is tight-lipped, and so I am. It looks as if nobody wants to lay a word on this topic. But the incident gives me a credit, a Meritorious Honor Award.

"For consistently demonstrating high level of performance, dedication and ingenuity in accomplishing tasks which has been outstanding and has substantially enhanced the effectiveness of the Anti-Fraud Unit."

I know all the while that Lucy is component of my award, and part of my life too. It's never easy to forget the woman who becomes a piece of one's life, at a very short time.

"I hope you're still alive and well. Wherever you are, I dedicate this credit to you, Lucy."

"You will have about 25 consular cases with you to finish in nine days," Mr. Scotch, our newly appointed Chief, said.

He is giving instruction to me and my colleague investigator, Homer, to do background investigation in the outlying provinces of Bicol region, about 300 miles away from Manila.

"Twenty five cases for nine days? We can't cope with the deadline, Boss," Homer said.

"Well, you have to, the car is scheduled for maintenance by that time," he said. "If you come back behind schedule it stands to reason that you're going sluggish in you jobs. You better prepare your cases now for your journey tomorrow."

Homer and I find it useless to argue with the chief. But we should abide by the instruction. On the contrary, we could still meet the deadline through hard works and added speed, considering two investigators doing 25 cases one at a time.

I'm the one driving the car while en route to the province. As we pass by the Alabang Center, I see my wife, Emma, at a crowded Bus Stop having a hard time taking a public bus going south. I almost forgot, she's going back home to our town in Sariaya, Quezon.

"Hey, Homer, can you see my wife?" I point my finger to her direction. He looked at the side mirror of the car.

"Oh, yeah, she's having a hard time taking the bus. Where is she heading to?" Homer said.

"..to our house in Quezon province," I said.

My wife looks helplessly struggling for a bus ride, almost causing her to be sideswiped by other incoming vehicles.

"Can we share her a ride?" I asked Homer, worried that my wife may possibly become a victim of an accident.

"Yeah sure, we're both going to the same direction in the south," he nodded.

We pulled over. "HEY! EMMA! Hope in!" I said.

She looks at our direction. Apparently, she's a bit surprise when she sees us. "Oh, there you are! Thank God you've seen me here, she said.

We resumed our journey with my wife on the backseat, and Homer on the front seat. Toward the last course of the south super hi-way at a running speed of about 80 to 90 mph, we had our right front tire blown-out in startling fashion. "BANG!"

The car swerved to the right as the wheel suddenly gone flat . I feel a bit of restriction. It feels like the steering wheel sticks a bit, forcing the car to sheer off course. I try to steer off back to the center of the road to gain momentum, but the flat tire is forcing the car to go off the highway and into the bumpy shoulder, making its way to crash against the huge electric post.

I put on the brake as hard as I can, forcibly steering its course to the left. The car then shrieks to a halt before it shaves the waiting electric post.

"SCREECH!" My forceful foot-brake has left four long tire-marks on the surface of the road before it finally stops.

"That's the first blow out we have had with this car," I told Homer while inspecting the damage. I find the blown out tire not reusable anymore. It's totally damaged. We work on it ourselves. There's no hope for a help at this point in time.

After fixing the spare tire with our supplied cross-bar, we continue to travel till we reach our family house in Sariaya town. Homer and I stay for a lunch as my wife prepares some foods.

We are talking about our trip when my neighbor knocks at the door. "Hi, hello Bruce!" I greet him first..

"I have an invitation card for you," he said.

What is it about?"

It's your godson's birthday, be there in my house." he told me while handing me the card.

"Oh, sorry Bruce, but we're set to leave for Bicol region, I'm afraid I can't," I said.

"Oh, come on, spare a day or two. Please, come!" Bruce insisted.

"Okay, I'll try." I accept the card and put it in our car compartment. I never have plan to stay longer. We have our cut-off date.

We left the house right after lunch. I did not tell Bruce. I do not want to waste time finishing the assignments to meet Mr. Scotch nine-day deadline, we would get ourselves into hot water for being late.

We reach Sorsogon province after nine-hour long drive from Sariaya, over rough terrains and into remote areas of the region. We check-in at a Travelers' Inn and spend a few days work, conducting background and neighborhood investigations of all twenty five questionable visa petitions that are still pending in the Anti-Fraud Unit.

On the seventh day we have been through with 22nd visa cases in both provinces of Albay and Sorsogon, and it rather looks good. We take too lightly that a few people in the neighborhood are holding against us. We never realize that some disappointed visa applicants together with their sympathizers are residents of the place and now they're plotting something for revenge.

"They're consular investigators, let's pounce on them when they come within reach."

"Yeah, we must knock them to the ground."

"The embassy turned me down last year because of them."

"They're collaborators; they're traitors! They don't care a hoot!" another man groaned.

"LET'S GET AFTER THE TURNCOAT!" The group assemble in a secluded pathway to lie in wait, holding bolos and clubs in their hands.

It's already 5:00pm and we decided to take a rest; go back to the inn for tomorrow's job.

"THERE THEY ARE!" one of the men shouts as he sees us getting into the car. The group run after us trying to hold us back, but we have already gotten into the car and I hastily start the engine. One of them grips my left arm and pulls me out of the car before the engine turns on, at the same time hacking me with a bolo. Homer is visibly silent in fear, he's stooping on the front seat.

"BOG!" The bolo hits the car door as I evade the attack. The blow leaves a deep straight mark on the edge of the car. I sidestep outside the vehicle and counter with a right hook on the chin, after which I quickly hop into the car--back to the driver's seat, locking the door and glass windows while the attacker is still mending the pain in his jaw. The rest of the men are gaining on us and the car engine couldn't start. We remain inside the car while I'm trying to start the engine. The group surrounded the car, each of them bares a furious look.

"GET OUT OF THE CAR!" one man yells, trying to force the door open.

At last, the engine starts right before the men could get through.

No time wasted, I drove the car fast to the direction of the next town, and down the rough road. The group gave chase.

"DRIVE FASTER! THE MEN ARE GAINING ON US!" Homer exclaimed and we left them behind. The men hurl us stones. One stone hits the back windshield of the car and it cracks down the middle.

"DON'T EVER COME BACK!" a man shouts while brandishing his fist. Homer sighs in relief when we finally reach the hostel.

"Almost!"he said.

"Well, that's part of our job; we do this for the sake of the service, don't we?" I told Homer. "Let's just prepare our things fast. We're leaving for Albay as soon as possible, those men must be chasing us by now."

We didn't waste time checking out. We travel in the middle of the night for Albay province and check in for a new hotel.

"We better while-away the night and talk about it over a glass of beer or two," I suggested to Homer while briefly resting in our hotel room.

"We still have three cases to do by tomorrow," Homer said.

"Anyway, our remaining cases are right here in Albay; in the surrounding vicinity. We can finish them up early in the afternoon tomorrow."

"Okay let's go!"

We are both seated at the back portion of a Sing-along Bar with a bottle of beer each, listening to a customer beside their table rendering an old song. Like him, we also want to sing along and just waiting for our turn.

"..And more, much more than this, I did it my way...!"

"HEY, HEY! ENOUGH! YOU'RE SINGING OUT OF TUNE!" a tipsy stranger yells at the singer to stop, but he just gives a fleeting look, he could not careless.

"I ate it up and spit it out," the song goes on.

"I SAID ENOUGH! The man stands up suddenly and draws near him, then pulls his gun out of his waist and aims at the singing customer to shoot.

"BANG!" the gun fired. The bullet makes its way to the ceiling of the bar as I instinctively grab the man's arm, dodging the gun out of the target before the shot. I subdue him by applying an Aikido lock to his wrist. The floor manager calls for the police and at no time they come over and arrest the gunman. "Thank you," the would-be victim told me.

The next day, we successfully finish investigating the three remaining cases in the vicinity of Legaspi City. We prepare to go back home to Manila, tired but happy because we are able to meet the deadline.

I am the one driving the car when I pull over.

"You drive," I told Homer.

All along I am the one driving and I want to share it with him. Probably I'm tired or something, so Homer must replace me. After all, he is also a professional driver, he is authorized to drive the diplomatic car.

While passing in the highland between cliffs and rough terrains, a black cat runs across our car and momentarily stands in the way, then slowly walks away to the other side of the road.

"It's a bad omen," I told Homer. "We must not continue travelling. There's a possible danger waiting for us out there."

That's my grandpa's superstitious belief, and mine too. The presence of the black cat crossing the road signals us to put paid to our travel back home.

 "But we have to get back to Manila to cope with the deadline," Homer insists.

"Alright, let's just put our seatbelt on," I suggested. We continued our trip with our seatbelt on anyway. It's seems to be a *smooth sailing*, but not for long. While running in moderate speed, our car suddenly went out of control and zigzagged the line from one side of the passageway to the other, then skidded off the cliff.

The car is thrown over the narrow chasm at a height of 30 to 50 feet above the sea level. I'm all shocked at the sight of our actual crash. My mouth wide-opened, my eyes deeply closed and I grimaced in fear. I'm not sure if I'm scared in the face of an imminent death, but probably, it's just my terrified reaction that I did nothing but shut my eyes in terror while our car is cradled by the wind; tense all my muscles in anticipation of my broken dead body, and for a split second, flashed back the memory of my nice olden days with my beloved family.

"MY KIDS!" I screamed on top of my voice as the vehicle went flying into the air and down below. The bark of a coconut tree is slightly shaved off in passing. The car hits the bottom of the cliff and turns right-side-down at sudden impact. The sound of heavy plunge breaks the quietude of the place. "CRASSHH!" Then, Silence...

THE AFTERMATH

Chapter 8

In Hot Water

Witnesses rush down the ravine and come to an aid. But thank God we are both alive; with simple bruises and no broken bones. Perhaps, the safety belts that we used in the car have just saved us from sure death. and perhaps, the ground below -- to where the vehicle tripped up right-side down, is soft enough to bear the impact of the crash. I thank God for saving my life.

While some local residents are coming to the rescue, Homer and I are talking nonsense. "Bimbo! BIMBO! ARE YOU ALIVE?" Homer said. He is slumped underneath the volume of baggage, partly covered with stock of files and everything in the car. I can't discern him.

"YES, I'M STILL ALIVE, HOW ABOUT YOU, YOU'RE ALIVE, AREN'T YOU?" I said.

That's a real nonsense! How can I ever answer him if I were dead? And how can I ask back that stupid question to a man who is just talking right now.

The people have just arrived down while we both come out of the fallen car. Obviously, they are amazed at the sight of our condition, we emerge unscathed. But somehow, they helped us climbing up to the top. We take a brief rest in front of a small store, just a few meters away from the cliff.

"How do you feel?" the store owner said.

"Well, I feel normal myself," I said.

"Here, you better have a drink," the storeowner said.

"Thank you." I feel thirsty and tired that I take the water for a drink. Right after gulping it down, I suddenly feel trembling of my muscles. My heart beats faster than it was before as if my chest is about to disintegrate. It continues beating for about an hour until it finally subsides.

"Something's wrong with the drinking water in your case," Homer said. "I think it's better not to take liquid immediately after the accident. I was correct I didn't dare drinking."

"Do we have to go back to the town proper to give a police report?" I asked.

"We've just traveled about three hours from the town; we'll spend another three hours going back to the precinct." Homer said. "The next town going back home to Manila is about 12 kilometers away, I think we could file our report to the local police in that place," I told Homer.

"That town doesn't belong to Camarines Norte, it's already in the Quezon province, and the police assigned there may not entertain us for juridical reason." We both argue deliberately on which way to go.

"Alright, we better wait for the first bus to come from either way. We'll take a ride wherever it heads."

"There it is!" the bus going back to Manila destination comes first, and then we take a ride. Without delay, we reach the next town of Calauag in Quezon province and alight from the bus. We look for the public phone and place an immediate long distance call to the Embassy.

"Hello Mr. Scotch," I said. " I'm sorry to inform you that we met an accident. Our car fell down the ravine."

"Oh my God, where is the car now? Are you alright?"

"Our car's still in the ravine, right-side down." I said. "We just left the car to let you know what happened," I'm a little bit restless.

"Where are you now?" "We're here in Calauag, Quezon. It's the nearest town from the place of accident. We're waiting for instruction if we should go back to the Camarines Norte police to file a report."

"No, you better proceed to your hometown in Sariaya, Quezon and take a rest. You should immediately consult a doctor about your physical condition."

"Okay, sir, thank you for your concern," I told Scotch. Unknown to me, Mr. Scotch contacted my telephone number in Sariaya. My sister-in law answers the phone call. And she said "Yes, yes." I don't know what are they talking about. I just learn it later. Here in Calauag, we are at the same time having an exchange of opinion. "I think we should be awarded from this accident," Homer told me.

"I think so." I told Homer. "The accident happened during our official tour of duty."

We reached my home through a passenger bus late at night. Homer went straight back home to Manila .the following morning; I consulted a doctor to follow Mr. Scotch' advice.

"That's only a few simple bruises, you're in excellent physical condition," the doctor said.

Although Mr. Scotch sounds sympathetic about our physical condition, I've had a dream the other night. I dreamed that something wrong is at hand. I saw myself sadly leaving the embassy, I was waving goodbyes to my colleagues. I even saw myself falling down the ground from the top of the building, and the people were laughing at my fall.

"You better consult a clairvoyant and ask what your dream is all about," my wife suggested.

Though I never believe in this kind of idiocy, I was finally convinced to visit a known clairvoyant in our community; after all, I have nothing to lose. Devin, the soothsayer set interview at the balcony of his house. I narrated him everything that transpired during the trip; and my nightmares. He placed his tarot cards on the table and recited his Latin prayer. He threw each card on the table and started reading the face.

"You never have to worry. You're in shape," he said.

"What about my future in the embassy?"

"They won't kick you out, you'll not be dismissed." Devin turns the face of another card.

"You're safe in your job. You will be promoted instead," he assured.

"How much?" I asked for his service fee.

"It's your show." I gave him One Hundred Pesos. I don't care whether it's stupidity or not, but somehow, I calmed down. My nightmares ceased from coming back.

The following day, Homer and I reported back to the office. We find it unusual that our colleague investigators are eerily silent on the issue. I began to smell a rat; I said "hi" to them, but they pretend not to hear us at all. That's strange. They don't even look at us as if they're busy working for nothing. It's not the way we expect them to treat us. Usually, they are always enthusiastic about how things are going on in the field.

Then I came to know later that right after my conversation with Mr. Scotch over the phone, he called a meeting and asked for the investigators' opinion regarding the previous incident.

'It's a pity that your colleagues met an accident in Bicol area," Mr. Scotch started the conversation.

"Are they hurt? Are they confined in the hospital?" Lazar, one of my colleagues, said.

"No," he said. "I send them back home to Sariaya. They called up from Calauag, Quezon. They left the car in Camarines Norte, at the place of accident."

"Well, maybe they're not present in the car during the actual accident." Demy, the most talkative and a pro-management investigator implied to Mr. Scotch.

"Somebody else should have driven the car."

"How come you ever conclude that?"

"You know, falling down the ravine is a serious matter. In effect, they should be injured and confined in the hospital. I can't imagine how they're able to proceed to Quezon province to call you up on that same day, whereas according to their story the accident happened in the other province?' can you just imagine that?" Demy said.

"Probably, they're somewhere else; in a party or something. Somebody could have borrowed the car while they're enjoying the party," Lazar butted in.

"You know the two of them are always fond of socializing." Apparently, my co-investigators are destroying us. To my mind, people of the United States are understanding. They always listen to what someone says and weigh one's words very carefully. But these two investigators are pulling us down. They're making us chickens coming home to roost. They are sinister, awfully sinister!

"I'll have this accident investigated," Mr. Scotch said, analyzing the dynamics of what he has heard of.

We worked on our investigation reports without a single word from our colleagues. Homer and I never talk to them either. I see trough the edge of my eyes their surreptitious looking at us. The Regional Security Office of the Embassy summoned us to investigate our case. I clearly described and explained what has truly transpired during the accident as much as I could remember.

While under office interrogation, other security investigators proceeded to the place of accident and even to my house in Quezon province. According to my informants, they went to the doctor who examined me in my town.

"Well, I find Poe some bruises, but it's okay, nothing serious," the doctor told the investigator.

"What about the pain in the chest and legs he's complaining about in the office?" the Investigator asked.

"Oh, he has been complaining such a problem before. I had him examined a month ago, he has a hypertension and rheumatism on both legs, it doesn't have to do with the accident in the car." They conducted background checks in our neighborhood. They asked some information from my friends. A close neighbor who used to be my drinking buddy whenever I'm home, even accompanied and helped them gather information about us, rather against us, whether or not I let somebody borrow the official car, or we're attending the party at the time accident. I'm not worried, I have a clear conscience. I'm just hopeful that the facts will finally come out. The accident is real, there' nothing else to cover up. After the investigators returned to the office, Mr. Scotch interrogated us in his room, one after the other. At close door, the chief was insistent.

"You're not in the actual scene when the car accident happened. Somebody's using the car. You were not there!" (Well, that's a leading question.)

"How come?" I said. "You can even ask and interview all witnesses in the place of accident. Show them our photographs and confirm who we are," I said.

"You know what we have found in the place?" Mr. Scotch pulled an invitation card and drags it to his desk.

"That card is in the compartment of the car. It's an invitation for you to attend a birthday party. You're actually partying in your town at the time of the accident," Mr. Scotch insisted. "You better confess so that I can help you," he said.

"What will I confess? It's really us falling down the ravine with the car!" I insisted.

"What about the invitation card, the date? July 20?" That's a clear evidence. The accident happened on the same day you're attending the birthday party."

"No I didn't." I blushed. "But yes, I accepted the card, but never we attended the party -- we're trying to beat your deadline," I told Mr. Scotch.

"You're lying!" Scotch yelled.

"May the lightning strike and hit my tongue!" I retorted.

"That's the normal speech of someone lying!"

"You do an injustice if you think I'm telling a lie." I snapped.

"The telephone operator called up your phone number and she asked your sister in-law if you're in the party, and she said yes, how can you ever explain that?" I try to calm down.

"My sister in-law, for your information sir, has hardly finished elementary. She's not used to talking to unfamiliar people on the phone. She used to say yes just to end the conversation. She's not used to too many questions either."

Mr. Scotch went off at a tangent. "You're using the official vehicle to transport an unauthorized passenger. That's willful, unofficial use of government vehicle."

"She's my wife," I said. " Homer and I were on our trip bound to the south. While on our way to Alabang Center we saw my wife at the bus stop, she's having a hard time taking a bus going back home to Quezon. She looked helplessly struggling to take a ride, and she's nearly sideswiped by an incoming vehicle. Fearing for a possible accident, I asked Homer for my wife to share a ride. After all, we were heading on the same direction, and he agreed with my suggestion."

"That's not a reason! You're not authorized to transport an unauthorized passenger, that's in the book," he said.

"Mr. Scotch," I said, "Can we consider that thing an infraction of the policy? We're at that time on official travel and we were also on official duty. Being diplomatic, every one of us investigators does the same thing when it comes to helping a helpless person whoever he is. But what about my wife? She's helpless, and it's my wife we're talking about here."

"That's still a violation of FSN handbook!" He maintained.

"But sir, granting that I allowed my wife to share a ride, it does only constitute an act which is purely humanitarian, a consideration to a helpless person. In a criminal case, any person who extends assistance to a helpless person under the impulse of uncontrollable fear of an equal or greater injury is exempt from criminal liability. In this particular case, the person who was allowed to ride was no less than my immediate wife and it is our human nature and inclination to act in defense of his loved ones. Our act is therefore justifiable, and such circumstances exempt us from liability or any nature of liability with the Embassy." I told Mr. Scotch.

But he is not satisfied. He probably doesn't want to buy my explanation, nor to the investigating officers' report. The recent accident is beginning to drive our "nail in the coffin." I was shocked to learn that the embassy to which I have given all due respect and loyalty continued to charge us of several violations in connection with that accident; one of which is the so-called "reckless driving resulting to damage to vehicle". This is so despite the fact that I was not the one driving the car when the accident happened. This is also true in spite of the fact that Mr. Scotch even insisted that we're not around when the accident occurred. How can you ever relate that?

"It appears that the action taken against us is so mean and improper, willfully motivated and self-serving," I've had this assumption.

The interrogation didn't stop there. Homer and I were even subjected to a hearing with the grievance committee and set the schedule of arraignment. We were advised to produce our own counsel. Ed, the security investigator on case recommended us a lawyer's name.

"He's the dean of the college of law," he said.

Homer and I found the lawyer's address in Quiapo, Manila, in the third floor of the building. Clients are waiting for their turn, and we waited for more than an hour before we become entertained. We laid our case and gave him a copy of our position paper clearly defining our stand

On the scheduled date of hearing, we even fetched him from his house and accompanied him to the embassy, hoping that he could give us a good defense.

"Attorney, do you bring a copy of our position paper?" I said while we are about to alight from the car.

"Huh! Did you give it to me? I haven't reviewed it yet." OH, MY GOD!

As we proceed to the chancery ballroom where the hearing is set to hold, our lawyer looked uneasy. He doesn't seem to be familiar with the place. Probably, it's his first time to face some diplomatic people of the embassy.

The conference room is occupied by heads of all the departments; NAMRU, JUSMAG, State Department, etc. All chairs around the long conference table are taken. The grievance committee panel started the deliberation for more than an hour. I'm certain that both of us, Homer and I, have clearly explained our sides. As I began to feel, the panel looked satisfied with our answers to their strongest questions.

"What about you Attorney? Do you have something to say?" one of them asked our counsel.

"Ah, yes," he stands up.

We feel very confident. Ed has just told us that our counsel is a dean of college of law and therefore, he must be a damned good lawyer. As he stands up, I thought he is going to batter a good defense by reciting some legal elaboration of the case. I thought he would articulate some points favorably to our argument, but I was absolutely wrong. He suddenly turned on me and stormed me with some irritating basic questions, right before the committee.

" Where were you during the time of the accident? What were you doing in the area? What did you do when you fell down the ravine?"

My God, he really didn't review our case -- he didn't study his lesson. He doesn't know anything about us. His way of questioning tends to show that he is groping on the issue, he wants to know the story first.

Members of the grievance committee are looking awry at him. I want to edge my shoes against his foot to try to stop questioning me that way, but doing so would surely catch the panels eyes. I decided to just keep silent. I'm really irritated of what he's doing. It's too academic. That's not the way we expected him to do.

The hearing finally ends up without us knowing the decision. We begin to imagine ourselves counting some public electric posts. We feel betrayed. The lawyer didn't do us any good. We should have not subscribed to Ed's recommendation. We should have known better.

"WE'RE IN HOT WATER!" Homer told me.

"Can we still be given a fair and righteous judgment over our case after this shame?" I said.

My only hope is the clairvoyant's prediction. I have always relied on it.

"You're safe in your job. You won't get fired. You will get promoted instead," the soothsayer assured me.

But I can't stop contemplating. I've always been staring at the framed awards hanging on my wall. Two Meritorious Honor Awards. One adopted Suggestion Award, a Special Achievement Award, and a Longevity Award of ten long years of services--with the U.S. Ambassador's picture shaking my hand. These are all official recognitions of my loyalty to the interest of the diplomatic mission.

MISCARRIAGE OF JUSTICE

Chapter 9
Out of the Frying Pan into the Fire

Despite our explanation with the grievance committee, we found ourselves finally dumped from the service for cause.

I could not help remembering my conversation with Homer the previous days.

"I believe we should receive an award from this accident,"

"Probably, yes we should. The accident happened during our official tour of duty."

That's all a punch to the moon!

One thing more, I'm now receiving unfair dealings from my old friends and kin.

"WHAT? It's unfair to you. You've done no wrong!" That's what they told me, but that's not what they meant to say. They do pretend to understand, but the truth of the matter is obvious--they are satisfied that I am now down and out.

"Birds of the same feather flock together."

I sure will now belong to the same poverty level. My intimate friends and next of kin who have always been enjoying my company have all fallen away like a flock of sparrows scared away by a lifeless, harmless scarecrow.

"Good for you!" That's the real phrase. My friends and kin showed their true colors as they laughed at me behind my back. Yeah, I know that.

I am now out of danger from my difficult assignments in the field--out of hatred from disgruntled Filipino countrymen who thought that I was a turncoat. But I'm still here in this world facing more dangerous and difficult situation because my entire life and the future of my family, especially my kids are completely at stakes. I am a victim of accident and become another victim of the embassy's miscarriage of justice. I'm *out of the frying pan into the fire*.

The labor code of the Philippines has ruled out that "any employee who is unjustly dismissed from the service except for just cause shall be entitled to reinstatement without loss of seniority rights and to full back wages, inclusive of allowances and to his other benefits or their monetary equivalent computed from the time his compensation was withheld from him up to the time of his actual reinstatement".

"That's what the labor law so states. But how could that be possible in my case?

Probably I could have done wrong somehow, but my spirit denies acceptance of any guilt. All I know is that I enjoy working with the embassy, with diplomatic people around me and all those challenging assignments that I love so much, that's why I did my job very well, and I did it with all my heart, my life and my soul, for my esteemed glory and for the interest of the service. But such unwanted car accident totally erased my dreams, suddenly refrained me from moving on, and most of all, the future of my children thus matters. Too bad we've been warned by the *black cat over the cliff* to discontinue our journey but we became stubborn and set it aside, thus, the accident.

The following day Homer and I complained our case to the Department of Labor. We want justice to prevail against such an unfair labor practices, but much to our dismay.

"This office doesn't have jurisdiction over your case," a labor official disclosed. "The embassy has diplomatic immunity and we can't help you out."

My goodness! We are legitimate, natural born citizen of this country and we do belong here. We were mistreated by a foreign management right in our own land and right on the face, and yet our own government couldn't do us anything. It *doesn't have a camel in the caravan.*

Frustrated and desperate, we proceed to the Department of Foreign Affairs for that purpose; to air our grievances. But we could not easily get into the concerned office. There are too many restrictions to follow. We finally decide to just place a call through a public phone. Luckily, a woman's voice responds to our call and entertains our complaint. I told her everything, from the time we went to the south, to the time of the accident until this separation from the service.

"Okay, ring me back about three days so we can give you the embassy's response concerning your complaint," the lady told me.

"Thank you, Ma'am. Bye!"

Three days flew fast after which I repeat my call to the foreign affairs following the lady's advice. I was able to connect with the same person of the same woman's voice.

"Hello Ma'am, this is Jeffrey Poe and I wish to make a follow up."

"Oh, well, Mr. Poe, I called up the embassy yesterday and I talked with the personnel department," she said.

"What did they say, Ma'am?"

"They told me that..." she paused for a few seconds. "you violated the embassy policy," she said.

"But Ma'am," I protest, "that's why we're here to air our side, we're illegally dismissed."

The answer is sarcastic. "Well, you better go there yourselves and explain it to them," she said.

I didn't expect that words from this foreign service personnel. For all we know, her job is to undertake negotiations; assisting Filipinos abroad (*well, I'm not abroad*) and protecting their rights; promoting Philippine culture and trade; bringing in foreign investments and promoting tourism to the Philippines; performing consular functions; and representing the Philippines in various international fora, among others.

Obviously, our first attempt to get diplomatic assistance has failed. It's disheartening to know that our very own government could not careless.

"My God, what's happening to our country?"

Exhausted but still hopeful, we continued our quest for justice.

We visited the Public Attorney's Office (PAO) and asked for any legal aid they could give, but the answer is just the same.

"We don't have jurisdiction over the embassy," the PAO lawyer told us. But he read our position papers, probably, just to lessen the gripes. He even interviewed us and shook his head after narrating him the story. "It shouldn't be that harsh! Granting that you really violate the policy, it's not worth the punishment. In my opinion, suspension should be enough but termination is too drastic.

"But, what shall we do, attorney?" I said.

"We can only file a request for reconsideration to the embassy, that's all we can do.

For a long week the lawyer burns his time working for our letter of reconsideration. He advised us to hand carry it, just to make sure that it will reach the concerned people in the embassy. The appeal letter has the Department of Justice heading address and we personally handed it to the reception personnel. (*I must thank the guard who allowed us to pass.*)

Months have passed by and we are impatiently waiting for the words coming from the embassy. There's no reply at all.

"The letter request is simply ignored," I told Homer.

"As a Foreign Service National who served the embassy with all loyalty and dedication, we've been dumped from the service for reason beyond our control. Too sad but our own government could not lend us a helping hand, " I said.

"Where shall we gather now?" Homer said.

"From here to inequity!"

Three months passed by without us seeing each other again. Perhaps Homer is too busy applying for a new job, but then I received a phone call from his cousin.

"HOMER IS DEAD!"

"HUH?"

"He died in desperation. But before he died, he sent words for you to carry on."

That's the last parting words. Homer, my colleague, probably in total desperation got sick and subsequently met his untimely death.

But I'm still fighting back. I have always wanted to keep alive. I don't want to be completely discouraged by this emotional trial and finally say farewell to the world in such a younger age of 40's, while leaving my bereaved family in future uncertainty. If we succumb to poverty, so be it! We shall be joined together in good times and bad times.

And bad time did occur.

Between Odds and Even

Chapter 10
The Final Chapter

"Poe! Wake up!" Emma is shaking my shoulder.

"What?" "Our kids are suffering high fever! They're chilling for cold," she said.

I leaped from the bed and prepared the kids to go.

"Let's rush them to the hospital!" We wrapped the kids with blankets and walked fast in the middle of the night, taking our children to the private road of the subdivision and over the bridge going to the hospital.

Obviously, my lingering trouble is timely compounded by such an ailment of these two young kids; Maybelle, a two-year age girl, and an eight-year age boy, Bimbo Jr. We chanced upon a private vehicle in the opposite direction and I waved my hand to stop the car hoping for a ride, but the driver ignored us. Both kids are in delirious situation and they are in need of immediate hospital attention. At the hospital, the receptionist performed a number of interviews instead of immediately confining the kids for medication.

Apparently, the hospital wanted to know if I could be able to pay the hospital bill. My youngest child experienced a seizure. The sudden stiffening and jerking of the little girl's muscles almost put me to frenzy.

"I have money! Stop interviewing me. The kids need immediate attention!" I shouted on top of my voice.

The doctor finally diagnosed that both kids are suffering Dengue fever in advance stage. Luckily we were able to rush them to the hospital at the wee hour of the night. The kids suffer exuberant pain. They are both inpatient on bed with bottle dextrose and tiny hose attached to their nose so as to flow out rotten dirt that looked like black decomposing human particles from their stomach. Other hose of dextrose are injected into their skin. The worst, the kids are not allowed to take any food or liquid and this punishment went on for several days. My kids are despondently wondering over my refusal to give them something to eat despite their repeated clamor for food.

"I'll go home for a while to get some clothes for the kids," I told my wife Emma.

"Be sure to come back here at once," Emma said.

At home, I was preparing lunch for the three other children when Emma called up.

"Come back here, Maybelle needs transfusing of blood, but the blood bank requires payment for the blood supply."

"The question of pay is not an important issue at the moment, I better go there now," I told Emma.

In a few minutes, I reached the hospital by a taxi and went straight to the blood bank to confront the head.

"My wife is requesting blood supply for my kid, but you refused to give it to her. Why, are you always after money? My kid is dying, and yet you still give importance to advance payment!" I was furious.

The head tried to explain, "Well, it's the hospital.."

"DAMN! If something happens to my kid, you'll have to suffer the consequence! I'll have you singled out in the newspaper."

He tried to calm me down, but I could not accept any explanation as long as the lives of my kids are at stake. To stop the frenzy, the blood officer beckoned his staff to release the blood supplies for my kid. Probably, I had some lessons to learn -- to fight on to attract immediate attention, and I'm damned right. The hospital blood bank is now attending to all my kids' blood prescriptions without delay.

"Her pulse is beating so weak and abnormally low," the doctor said after checking Maybelle's condition.

"Hurry, hand me a cup of coffee -- a real strong coffee," the doctor told the nurse. The coffee is forcibly inserted into my little girl's mouth for her to swallow. She has a blank look. The pupils of her eyes are slowly turning white.

At the adjacent ward, my son Bimbo Jr. is also lying flat on the bed, obviously weaker but still conscious..

"Mama, please read this bible for me," he told his Mother.

"MY GOD!" My heart is melting a hundred times! It's the most challenging moment in my life. Both kids are in 50-50 condition and I'm not sure if I could withstand the fear of saying sad farewell to my kids. In any moment, they might finally be leaving us forever.

"LORD, I NEED YOUR HELP!"

In my hopeless moment, I went outside the hospital to buy a bottle of brandy and gulped down the whole content without let-up. Between drink and worries, I am constantly appealing to the Lord harder and ever -- to spare my kids from the toil of death and to send them hasty recovery instead.

I do not know if it's an effect of brandy, but suddenly, I felt a strange spirit creeping into myself, more burning than the spirit of brandy I gulped down awhile ago to reinforce my emotional strength. It's a very splendid feeling I have never felt before.

"MY CHILDREN?" I rushed back to the hospital, so worried that I almost fly into the ward in four big leaps.

But my lingering trouble paid off. I found my kids in recovering condition. My wife has refrained from crying, and the doctor as well as the nurse are standing before my kids with their normal face.

"The little girl's pulse is recovering, it's now beating normally," the doctor told me. And Bimbo Jr.? He is calmly reading a few bible verses himself.

"Thank you God! You haven't forsaken us! You still have your mercy for us to be heard of and for us to ask for forgiveness." AMEN.

It's a very torturing and wonderful experience. First, I was unlawfully dumped by the embassy. Second, my two kids almost died of serious, dangerous ailment.

But on the other hand, it's a wonderful experience that I have proven one more time that God is always there to lend me a helping hand. The children have finally recovered and ready to go out of the hospital anytime.

But I was not through with my dilemma.

"Before you can go, please pay your hospital bills at the cashier section," the receptionist told me while the bill clerk was handing me the statements.

I went down to the nearest bank to encash the last check I got from the embassy. That's more than enough to pay our bills--to leave the hospital as soon as possible, but much to my dismay.

"Sir, this check needs clearing for a one-month period. You can't encash it today.

I don't have available cash in my purse. I can't be able to pay the bills right away. The only thing I have is the check in my hand representing my total separation pay.

The kids were forced to extend days in the hospital waiting for their release.

My wife has been telling me to seek help from my siblings, but I refused her. I know for a fact that they would only turn us down. She volunteered to go despite my refusal, bringing with her the embassy check as a ready collateral.

"Emma, I have my cash available here," my sister said. "But I can't risk the money for your kids because you might not be able to pay me in time. It's intended for my son's wedding next month."

Hopeless and disappointed, my wife visited my eldest brother.

"Where on earth can I have that big amount of money?" he is visibly angry. "It's your fault you confined your kids in the expensive hospital!"

That's a dumping word. It really hurts. My wife went out of the house in great tears. My brother, he is
 not only refusing us to give a helping hand, he's even blaming us in our predicament. He's adding insult to the injury.

My wife went back to the hospital with a heavy heart.

"They turned me down," Emma told me in a low voice. "I told you so, you won't get them to change their mind-set," I scolded my wife.

I also feel my grudges. It grieves me to see my wife in such pain. In fact I can no longer hide this frustration over this kind of treatment we get from my very own family.

"My friends and kin have forsaken me. I can no longer think of anyone who could extend us help," I told Emma.

"Let us pray!" she said.

We were both seated on the edges of the hospital bed mending our problem when an unexpected visitor came by.

"Hello, how are the kids, uncle?" It's Ofell, Emma's niece.

"They're okay now, but they can't be released unless we pay the hospital bills."

"It's okay now, don't you worry; I have money to lend. The kids can go back home now," she said.

My wife and I had a surprised exchange of look. We couldn't believe our eyes. "Oh, Wow! Thank you, Ofell, You're an angel!" Emma couldn't hold out her tears.

Once, I branded her as a selfish woman.

"Selfish people are self centered and always looked at life as if they are the center of the Universe. It is very difficult to get along with selfish people because they are always willing to take and never willing to give".

But now Ofell is actually in here, right before my kids, volunteering to lend us a helping hand. This could be a great turn of event. I remember God's word:

"Now this I say, he who sows sparingly will also reap sparingly, and he who sows bountifully will also reap bountifully. 7Each one must do just as he has purposed in his heart, not grudgingly or under compulsion, for God loves a

cheerful giver. 8And God is able to make all grace abound to you, so that always having all sufficiency in everything, you may have an abundance for every good deed".

Ofell, the last person I could think about when it comes to money, is now offering her help, voluntarily and unexpectedly.

Again, it's the hands of God that matter. After all, it's an eye opener to me.

"Never trust a new found friend any further than you can throw them". Never take somebody by how they look. What matters is what's inside their soul, their heart, their feelings. In short, "Don't judge a book by its cover".

I've gone to have dangerous job in the field of investigation, and I had no idea what made it so dangerous. All I knew was that I was determined to perform my job with utmost loyalty and dedication, but the silliest accident wouldn't allow me to continue. I was broken into pieces.

But now, after six months of killing my time carrying a big stone in my heart, my firmness finally pays off. I've got a new job--away from such a dangerous assignments and discrimination.

My colleague Investigators? They were also kicked out for reason unknown to me.

What process could be better than seeking the convivial arms of the Divine Providence at times of trouble and at times when one had sorted to all recourses but they didn't seem to work at all?

Anything beyond the capability of man should be consigned into the custody of the Lord.

As Jesus said, "Come to Me all you who are weary and heavy-laden, and I will give you rest" (Matthew 11:28).

"It's not rejection that people fear, it is the possible consequences of rejection. Preparing to accept those consequences and viewing rejection as a learning experience that will bring you closer to success, will not only help you to conquer the fear of rejection, but help you to appreciate rejection itself". – Anonymous

I'm all better now. I can no longer fear the pain.

"THANK GOD!"

AMEN.